The Cheapskate's Guide to
Entertaining

The Cheapskate's Guide to Entertaining

✦ ✦ ✦

How to Throw Fabulous Parties on a Modest Budget

LORI PERKINS

A Citadel Press Book
Published by Carol Publishing Group

Copyright © 1999 Lori Perkins

A Citadel Press Book
Published by Carol Publishing Group
Citadel Press is a registered trademark of Carol Communications, Inc.

Editorial, sales and distribution, and rights and permissions inquiries should be addressed to Carol Publishing Group, 120 Enterprise Avenue, Secaucus, N.J. 07094.

In Canada: Canadian Manda Group, One Atlantic Avenue, Suite 105, Toronto, Ontario M6K 3E7

Carol Publishing Group books may be purchased in bulk at special discounts for sales promotion, fund-raising, or educational purposes. Special editions can be created to specifications. For details, contact Special Sales Department, 120 Enterprise Avenue, Secaucus, N.J. 07094.

Manufactured in the United States of America
10 9 8 7 6 5 4 3 2 1

Library of Congress Cataloging-in-Publication Data

Perkins, Lori.
    The cheapskate's guide to entertaining : how to throw fabulous
parties on a modest budget / Lori Perkins.
        p.   cm.
    ISBN 0-8065-2038-8 (pbk.)
    1. Entertaining.   2. Consumer education.   I. Title.
TX731.P384   1999
642′.4—dc21   98-35548
                                                                        CIP

To my dad,
Who taught me the fine art of frugality

And to my mom,
Who taught me the love of entertaining

Contents

Preface

All my life I've been a tightwad. It's a personality trait I acquired from my dad, who did the family food shopping and knew no greater thrill than double coupons and "buy one, get one free." He sought out early-bird dinner specials and restaurants that served a free glass of wine or after-dinner drink with the meal. He taught me to wait until the holiday sales to make big purchases (such as cars and appliances), to travel off-season whenever possible, and to comparison-shop on every item I could ever want, including my college education and my wedding.

My mother taught me the joys of entertaining. We have a large extended family and have always had family get-togethers for the holidays, even when times were tight. My parents had a large crowd of friends whom they entertained at least once a year at what I thought of as elegant cocktail parties. I loved to watch my mother putting together trays of mushroom and sausage hors d'oeuvres that we weren't allowed to touch.

I went to a fancy private school (on scholarship, of course) where the birthday parties were held at Broadway shows and midtown-Manhattan hotels, but my mom managed to throw me equally impressive parties at a fraction of the cost of those of my classmates by being more creative than my friends' parents. Even before I had a place to host parties, I was throwing them for my teenage friends when my parents would go away for the weekend. I would put together disgusting punches based on two bottles of Southern Comfort (which, in addition to being all I could afford, was known to be potent) and vats of onion dip and chips.

It was only natural that when I became a young adult and moved out on my own, I was the party girl. Of all my friends, I could always be counted on to throw the Halloween party, the annual New Year's Eve party, and the Thanksgiving feast, even though we all made less than squat (we were all starving journalists).

As newlyweds, my husband and I continued the tradition of the New Year's Eve party; we threw my brother his going-away-to-California party and even organized a treasure hunt throughout Manhattan for our friends one summer. I threw my parents a surprise twenty-fifth wedding anniversary party (my Dad nearly had a heart attack, so the surprise part was not such a good idea) and my husband and I each gave the other a thirtieth birthday party (plus I threw him a surprise thirty-fifth). We're parents now, so we do our child's birthday party, as well as the annual holiday gatherings for the extended family and a whole summer of weekend barbecues for our friends, because we live in New York City in a co-op with a pool and most of our friends have no place to swim.

Over the course of the year, we host about ten parties and another dozen dinner gatherings. Most are simple and intimate dinners at home for fewer than twelve people, but this year I threw an office party for 120, as well as a very complicated child's birthday party for fourteen children and their parents with an *Indiana Jones and the Temple of Doom* theme.

I love to entertain, and I love being the one to bring all my friends and family together for a good time. Even though we are a two-income family, we could never throw the parties we do if we didn't plan everything and squeeze blood from stones to put everything together.

Not everyone is a natural cheapskate, but few of us can afford to do all the things we want without pinching pennies here and there. It takes a certain mind-set to constantly figure out ways to save money, but it is one that can be easily learned.

Many of my friends say they can't afford to entertain as much as we do, but that's because they overdo it and exhaust both their financial and time budgets in doing so. Entertaining is an important part of who I am, so I actually budget it into my life. I plan to entertain on a regular basis and am therefore not surprised by how much it costs or how much time it takes to prepare and clean up.

I know that we will be hosting at least twenty-five get-togethers a year, so I always keep my kitchen well-stocked and buy entertainment-oriented items such as paper plates and plastic cutlery in bulk. If I had to, I could throw together a dinner party for sixteen or a buffet for thirty at the snap of a finger on next to nothing, or for less than $25.

One time I did have to. We had hosted a christening luncheon for our son, and several members of the immediate family came back to the apartment with us and stayed until dinner, for which I was roasting a relatively small leg of lamb (to serve eight). I threw on pots of rice and made a killer salad and ended up feeding at least sixteen people, and I made it all look effortless.

The goal of this book is to make entertaining so affordable and effortless—and thus enjoyable—that you can't imagine a weekend without some kind of party!

The Cheapskate's Guide to
Entertaining

1

The Basics
of a Successful Party

It is easy to entertain extravagantly. There are very few guests who would not enjoy a meal of filet mignon, caviar, and fine champagne. There are also very few of us who can afford to serve that meal to more than six people more than once or twice a year. I wouldn't want to either, because it would be the luxuriousness of the ingredients, and not my contribution to them, that would make the biggest impression.

For me, the success of any gathering is in the personal details—the place (I've chosen to invite you to my home), the choice and distinct flavor of the food, the ambiance, decor, and company. With enough planning and careful attention to detail, you can make any party seem truly extravagant without spending yourself into bankruptcy.

I strongly believe that all gatherings should have a theme. It gives a unifying concept to your party and a direction for your creativity. A theme makes it easier for you to decide what to cook and how to decorate, as well as how to set the tone for your gathering. It gives the hostess a focus around which to plan the perfect personal details.

When I look back on the most memorable dinners and parties I've attended, I rarely remember whether or not the hostess served on Limoges china or had a Waterford crystal punch bowl. It was often the simplest things, such as a homemade ethnic feast or a special event, like a treasure hunt, that made a lasting impression.

Years of hosting parties have taught me that various decisions must be made and carefully thought out well in advance. For example, do you want to have a sit-down or a buffet dinner or a cocktail party? Is there a theme for the party? What is the basic menu? Do you want to have any special ambiance and decor? Once you have decided upon these party basics, then you move on to the organization and budgeting of the party.

Deciding What Kind of Party

For me, the kind of party I'll choose to have depends on the number of people I can fit comfortably into my apartment and how much work I want to do once my company arrives. I can fit twelve adults at my dining table and a children's table very comfortably, so sixteen is my maximum for a sit-down dinner, though there is the option of placing another table in my living room and rearranging furniture. I once attended a sit-down Christmas dinner where the furniture had been completely removed from one room, and four tables were placed in an open square to seat forty, which worked quite well.

For more than fifteen people, and up to thirty, I would have a buffet dinner, where I present the food on my dining room table. I might add a small table or two for drinks or dessert. This way, I can still serve sumptuous meals that come in individual portions, such as a carved roast or chicken parmigiano.

For more than thirty people, and up to a maximum, for my home, of sixty (which is the maximum I would recommend for the the average three-room entertainment area of interconnecting dining room, kitchen, and living room), I would host a cocktail party. This would require at least two large tables set up at opposite ends of the party area, with small tables of finger food distributed throughout.

Deciding on the Menu and Theme

Most of the gatherings we host are for a specific occasion, such as a birthday or holiday. Many of them come with a preplanned menu because of family tradition (turkey on Thanksgiving, lamb or ham on Easter) or because they always fall at a certain time of the year (someone's summer birthday is always a barbecue). However, it is easy to vary the menu or the theme with just a little creativity. If you find yourself hosting a number of Christmas gatherings, for example, try something like a Christmas fiesta, where you serve Mexican food and perhaps feature a Christmas piñata for the children.

The theme can be expressed by something as simple as deciding to have Italian food (antipasto, a pasta dish, and Italian pastries supplemented by an Italian wine and music) or as complicated as hosting a vegetarian low-fat birthday for someone with a health problem (grilled fish and vegetables and angel food birthday cake with white and gold accents and perhaps an angel motif).

Putting together the theme of a dinner or party is relatively easy. It's just a matter of coordinating the food and decor and ambiance according to some unifying concept. As in the examples above, you can do this by choosing to serve a certain type of food (French, Chinese, Mexican), by occasion (holiday or birthday), by season (barbecue or picnic), or by an idea you come up with on your own (a '70s or a *Star Trek* party). You then go through the basic elements of a party, such as food, decor, and entertainment, to make sure that they all coordinate.

While the food I serve is often decided by the theme of the party, I try to also take into consideration what's on sale seasonally, such as fresh-picked apples in the fall or basil or blueberries in the summer. Turkey and leg of lamb are more readily available around the holidays (less expensive, too). The supermarkets that I frequent have a once-a-year sale on lobster at $4.99 per pound (it regularly sells for somewhere between $7.99 and $11.99 per pound in New York) and tuna steak for $3.99 per pound (again, regularly somewhere between $7.99 and as much as $13.99 per pound), so if either of these are on sale, I might make a paella with the lobster or grill the tuna steak and serve it over pasta with olive oil and garlic. Sometimes I base the theme on the food, instead of the other way around.

Decor and Ambiance

Once you know what you are going to serve, it is easy to set the table. As long as you remember to keep an eye open for beauty, you should be able to put together a unique and decorative table using color, texture, and creativity, without spending a lot of money. A well-set table should feature a centerpiece of some sort (this can be very simple), a table covering (this does not need to be a traditional table linen), and accents, such as candles and candlesticks.

Your home should reflect your taste and style. If you are comfortable with your home, your guests will be too. Never try to present a style that is not comfortable for you. For instance, if there is not a single white feature in your home decor, your should not feel compelled to run out and buy white table linens. You'll be more comfortable if you find a tablecloth that reflects your taste. The same goes for china and flatware.

I have found that the table centerpiece can often be put together from the food you are serving. A basket of highly polished apples or a bowl piled high with summer fruit is as beautiful as an antique vase of pink roses. In the fall, I often put together a centerpiece of autumn vegetables, such as squash, pumpkin, and corn, around a basket of fresh-baked bread. For Easter, I place hand-dyed Easter eggs in a ceramic basket as the table's centerpiece.

Because I often set my table centerpiece from what I am serving, I have made a habit of collecting baskets—from my son's Easter basket rejects to those that come as gifts with toiletries. Lined with a linen napkin, or even a colorful dishcloth, they make wonderful accents when filled with bread, fruit, wildflowers, colored eggs, or holiday cookies. Near the holidays (which includes Valentine's Day), you can pick up almost any size or variety (from unvarnished to gold-sprayed) basket at the dollar stores.

I have also collected a number of bowls, from a large pasta bowl to small condiment-size dishes. I try to find them in colors and patterns to complement my everyday dishes, but I will also buy glass or crystal dishes, because they go with everything. I have a special four-section glass dish in which I serve olives and pickles, and I use it almost every time I entertain.

For a table covering, you can use the more traditional lace or linen tablecloths. However, more creative table coverings such as a hand-made quilt or large piece of fabric (batik or even muslin) or color-coordinated materials to go with the holiday or season (red and green for Christmas or pastel for spring or Easter) make very nice accents. Some hostesses choose to dress up a plain table with a decorative runner, which can be a seasonal or colorful pattern.

Table accents can be as simple as matching candlesticks, whether family heirlooms or dollar-store finds. Ceramic figurines are also a nice touch for holidays, and they can be as expensive as Lladró or as inexpensive as pilgrim figurines found in an outlet store.

I also have a few nice vases (one was a wedding gift, one a flea-market find, and one I made—see chapter 3) in which I will occasionally place seasonal flowers. I love to display pussy willows in the spring and wildflowers all summer. A few well-chosen silk flowers (which I have seen on sale at the dollar store) make a good invest-ment for last-minute decorating.

In addition to dressing up a table with food-filled baskets, large seashells make interesting holders for condiments. Some caterers swear by hollowed-out red and green peppers or purple cabbages as bowls to hold dip.

I have invested in some nice salt and pepper shakers (a crystal set, as well as silver), as well as a handful of seasonal shakers (for Christmas, Halloween, Thanksgiving, and Easter), because they also dress up the table.

Music is important to set the tone of the evening, but it should always be in the background, unless you are having a party with dancing. For ambiance, I often play classical music or jazz, but I will always play holiday music when appropriate.

If the basic elements of your party are well thought out and you are proud of them, you will give off an air of confidence, which will ensure that your guests are comfortable. When your guests are happy and you are self-assured, your party is bound to be a success!

2

The Basics of Frugal Entertaining

The single most essential way to save money is to *plan ahead*. While it is possible to throw a much-talked about party on a whim, you're bound to spend much more than you have to if you don't take the time and make the effort to think everything out in advance.

Attention to detail is the second most important element of successful entertaining on a budget. You must cover all the entertaining basics, and then pick one or two party elements and really splurge there, such as on a fabulously rich dessert or a complicated appetizer. Your guests will remember for years that you served home-made stuffed artichokes or a lush array of strawberries dipped in chocolate and never recall that the china didn't match or that your glasses weren't crystal. Choosing the right details with which to make your personal entertaining statement is essential.

When to Start Planning

A month is a good time frame to give yourself, although I often plan for annual parties (my son's birthday) or holiday get-togethers all year 'round. By this I mean I begin clipping coupons for the holiday feasts in August; I often buy holiday accents the day after the holiday, when they are usually half price (tablecloths, candles, salt and pepper shakers, ceramic figures); and, once my son has decided on the theme for his annual party (Batman, Aladdin, Power Rangers, Indiana Jones), I immediately begin collecting party favors and assorted paraphernalia.

Allowing yourself a month also gives you enough time to send out invitations and get back responses, so that you'll know how many people will be coming. There is nothing more embarrassing than not having enough food, beverages, or party favors and running out to the store at the last minute. On the other hand, you don't want to get stuck with too much food that you can't return and six extra party bags for five-year-olds.

A month also gives you ample time to shop around to get the best buys on the things you will need and to look for those "just-so" details that will make your party stand out. It should also give you enough time to set up the help you might need.

The Importance of Lists

Make lists of everything that's involved in planning the party. Don't expect that you'll just *remember* to go out and get ice the day of the party or that your friend will remember to return your big salad bowl. You need lists to plan the menu and figure out how much food you'll need, as well as how much liquor, soda, and ice to have on hand. Make sure you have enough dishes and cups (with extras for refills), flatware, table linens and napkins, garbage bags, and paper towels.

You also need to make lists to help you plan your decor, if you are going to need any centerpieces, candlesticks with candles, banners, or party favors. This is especially important if the party is for a special occasion (you do not want to be searching for birthday candles at the last minute).

Be absolutely sure to make a list of things to do the day of the party and the order in which you will do them. This ensures that you won't forget some detail like putting the beer on ice, and that you won't be in the middle of setting the table when the doorbell rings.

Budgeting Time and Money

You have to set realistic budgets for both time and money, and have a fallback plan (such as taking off work the day before the party if necessary) in case either one of these projections goes dreadfully wrong at the last minute. It is my firm belief, and one that has been proven true throughout my party-throwing life, that you can get anything you want or need at a discount if you just take the time to shop around. However, this may mean going to ten different stores and then back again for the best price. Only *you* know if it's worth it.

I do a lot of my bargain shopping over the phone ("Do you have Batman invitations? How much are they?"), so I don't have to go from store to store. You'd be surprised how easy it is if you know the right places to call, but making the calls takes time too. I have a busy day job, so sometimes I bring my local phone book to the office and make those calls during my lunch hour. I try to buy as much as possible *before* the weekend of the party.

Liquor is often the most expensive element of a gathering, so the type and quantity of drinks you serve will largely determine how much you spend overall. Champagnes and expensive wines might be what you choose to splurge on, but you can make just as impressive a statement by serving a champagne punch or an unusual wine (such as Beaujolais Nouveau, which arrives in the States in November) or make pitchers of mixed drinks. You can always buy alcohol by the case or in larger bottles (and serve in decanters or pitchers, so your guests don't know that you bought the four-liter jug of sangria) to reduce costs for a large party. This is also the one area where you don't have to be afraid to overbuy: most liquor stores allow you to return unopened bottles of liquor.

The main course is the second biggest factor determining the cost of the party. Expensive cuts of meat and shellfish will cost you a pretty penny, but you can save money if you look for sales. (Get friendly with your butcher and he or she may tell you about sales ahead of time.) Other ways to save are by buying in bulk (sides of beef to freeze, large quantities of filet mignon or shell steak, roast your own pig), cutting your own meat (whole chicken is cheaper than chicken breasts), or buying frozen. Frozen African lobster tails or Chilean shrimp are fine for something like paella. You can also buy one expensive ingredient, such as crab or smoked salmon, and stretch it out by serving it in a pasta dish, soup or bisque, or a salad as the main course. I once had a filet mignon salad that was out of this world.

Appetizers and dessert are usually not budget busters, but you can choose to splurge here with something like caviar and Brie appetizers on toast points (a little caviar and a lot of Brie) or some truffle or hors d'oeuvres. Some desserts are more expensive to make than others, such as those that require liqueurs (but you can buy small bottles) or out-of-season fruits. (Try finding raspberries or fresh pineapples in February.)

Budgeting time to shop properly and to make all these exquisite menu features is essential. When I entertain, I only have one or two difficult and/or time-consuming menu items, which I prepare the day before (usually the dessert, maybe the bread). I make a lot of batches of things all year long, such as pesto and pie crusts and sugar cookie dough, so I can just defrost it when the time comes. I like to save the day of the party for setting up and preparing the main course.

Where to Shop

I live in New York City, so the world is my oyster, but the places I shop for party goods can be found throughout the country, especially in suburbia. One year I found the entire party setup for my son's Aladdin-themed birthday at a party store that was going out of business while on vacation in Florida. I bought the whole lot (centerpiece, table-cloths, invitations, goodie bags, balloons, and blowers) and carried it back to New York in a shopping bag. My husband thought I was crazy, but my son was in his glory, and the party was a big success because the details were perfect (the other moms were amazed that I had managed to find a genie piñata). This year I found leather bullwhips for the Indiana Jones party at a dollar store in Maine. Details, details.

I go to different stores for different kinds of party items such as food, beverages, linens and tableware, and party decorations, although I could probably get everything I needed at my local supermarket and pay a lot more.

For food and soda, I usually go to a wholesale membership club like Costco or Sam's or BJ's. I find that the annual membership fee is far less than what I save by shopping there, especially since I host a number of parties every year. (I also buy household items and my son's lunch supplies in bulk all year 'round.) However, if you don't think the savings will cover the membership fee (usually between $25 and $50 a year), you can ask around to see if one of your friends will take you shopping on her membership card or share a membership with a friend. (This is another reason for planning ahead, because if you are asking someone for a favor, you have to do it on her schedule.)

I find these wholesale clubs are great for getting large amounts of food, especially the more expensive cuts of meat and fish and fancy ready-made appetizers (smoked salmon, hummus, paté, wheels of cheese). They're also good for fruit and vegetables in bulk. I often buy Italian bread, pita, and French bread and freeze them for the day of the party.

These stores are also a good place to buy assorted crackers, but I find I can sometimes get better deals at a supermarket on the better brands of chips and snacks. This is an area where you have to comparison-shop.

Some wholesale clubs feature hors d'oeuvre platters, from shrimp cocktail to crudites with dip, which can really save you time and money, but you must buy them the day of the party.

Costco doesn't sell liquor in New York, so I go to a Costco in New Jersey for party liquor. (There is also no bottle deposit in New Jersey, so I save on cases of soda and/or beer, and the sales tax is slightly less.) Call ahead of time to find out if your wholesale club sells alcohol. If not, look in your local phone book for the discount beverage wholesaler nearest you. Call first to find out if they sell to the public, if they have what you want, and what methods of payment they take. Some of these places may even deliver and take your order over the phone (that way you save time and money).

Of course, I go to supermarkets for most of my everyday food needs (dairy products, flour, coffee, tea) and some of my meat. I prefer to go to a greengrocer for my fruits and vegetables, because they have more variety and the produce is cheaper and fresher. For instance, I can always get six lemons for $1 at the local greengrocer, whereas they're 79 cents at the supermarket. Bags of potatoes and onions are less expensive, as are herbs and spices.

Go to a specialty or gourmet store (such as Zabar's or Balducci's in New York) only for specific items, such as gourmet coffee beans or a hard-to-find cheese or spice. Supermarkets generally have extensive sections of ethnic food where you can usually find the basic ingredients for Latin, Greek, Italian, Thai, Chinese, and Japanese food. Many Italian specialty ingredients, such as marinated mushrooms, peppers or artichoke hearts, and pine nuts, can be found in bulk at a wholesale club. For specific ethnic ingredients, I prefer to go a local ethnic shop such as a Greek grocer or an Italian deli, where these items are more likely to be realistically priced.

I am addicted to 99-cent or dollar stores, where every item in the shop is a dollar or less. I have never been to a state that doesn't have one, and I travel extensively throughout the East and the West coasts every year. Most are in malls and have the words "dollar" or "99 cents" in their name (such as the Dollar Queen in Maine or Jack's 99 Cents in midtown Manhattan). Do not be shy about asking friends, family, or mall workers where the nearest 99-cent store is (they've even sprung up in England as 99-pence stores).

I know where every 99-cent store is in a twenty-five-mile radius of my home and office. When I'm planning a party, I usually case these places once a week for things like themed plastic plates and kids' party favors for a buck because their stock changes constantly since they sell closeouts. If they don't have it one week, it may be there the next. They're great for adult party favors too, and even wedding mementos.

However, when I'm planning a big birthday or event party, I also visit my local party warehouses. They often have terrific party goods at half price, as well as trinkets and mementos that are even cheaper than what you might get at a dollar store. Look up "party store" in your yellow pages to find one.

I also cruise Kmarts, Wal-Marts, Walgreens, Bradlees, Caldors, T.J. Maxx, Ross, Odd Lots, Webers, Rock Bottoms, MacFrugals, and other stores that sell discount merchandise, especially closeouts. I never pass an outlet store without seeing how deep the discount is. I put myself on mailing lists too—manufacturers (such as IKEA and Dansk, which are both great for housewares) will often notify you of sales and sometimes send you coupons for 10 or 20 percent off. These places are great for holiday table linens and accents. You can find these stores in the local phone book or call directory assistance for the stores in your area code or the 800-number area code for directory information.

Another great way to buy party favors and knickknacks in bulk, or by theme, is through catalogs. I'm not crazy about paying the delivery charge, but if the price or the detail is right, it can be worth it.

Novelty catalogs, such as Oriental Trading and Archie McPhee, have great party favors for kids (100 erasers for $1.99, Ping Pong eyeballs at 7 cents each) and there are some catalogs that sell merchandise in threes for deep discounts, such as LTD Commodities and ABC. Catalogs are also a dependable way for you to find offbeat items like drink parasols and Hawaiian leis in the middle of winter at a reasonable price.

Coupons

I keep a coupon file, and I have a section for party items. This is usually where you have to buy more than one item to get $1 off, or you buy one and get one free. These aren't useful for my regular shopping, but when I know I'm having a number of people over, it's great to get two cheese spreads for the price of one.

The categories of food that I am most likely to find coupons for are juices and soda, chips and snacks, dips, cheese spreads, and dessert. I always clip the candy coupons, because I use kisses, M&M's, and Reeses Peanut Butter cups as accents at parties where kids will attend. I love the Ferrero chocolate coupons, and try to save them up for use in a store that features double coupons.

Occasionally, you'll find a coupon for $1 off a Butterball turkey, smoked sausages, hot dogs, bacon, or a line of cold cuts, such as Healthy Choice. Perdue always offers some coupons on their chicken breasts.

There are many coupons for frozen desserts and ice cream. I clip them all on the off chance that I may have to buy something at the last minute. There are also numerous coupons for ice cream cakes at Carvel and Baskin-Robbins, which are great for kids' parties (or for husbands who need to feel like a kid once in a while).

If you know you are having a party and you see a coupon for a menu item in the local flyer, there is nothing wrong with calling a family member or friend who knows and respects your frugal streak and asking him or her to clip the coupon for you, so that you can buy fifty Nathan's hotdogs for the price of twenty-five. I have often based a meal on a fantastic two-for-one deal (two pounds of feta cheese or smoked turkey breast for the price of one) at the local supermarket.

My local supermarket also offers free food with the purchase of $100 worth of groceries at certain times of the year. One year I "earned" a free turkey (at Christmas), smoked ham (Easter), and a five-pack of matzoh (Passover). One year they offered a picnic for eight with hot dogs and buns for the Fourth of July. I froze all of these things and eventually used them to entertain.

Although they're not technically coupons, I believe strongly in discount cards—credit card–like store shopping cards that give you discounts on selected items at the cash register while allowing the supermarket to track your purchases. I have cards in every supermarket I shop in so that I can get the "clip-less" coupons that are offered each week. Coupled with a brand-name newspaper coupon, you can sometimes get terrific deals for as little as 25 cents.

Bartering and Borrowing

I'm a great fan of barter, and by this I mean exchange of services. For example, a friend who makes a wicked German chocolate cake will bake you one in exchange for your baby-sitting her three kids one afternoon. You'd be amazed at what you can barter if you set your mind to it. Sometimes by bartering you're giving someone a chance to hone their skills and use you as a future reference. (Let's say a neighbor's teenager is learning jazz guitar and you could use some musical entertainment . . .)

I also believe in borrowing with payback, but the payback can be in services or a future IOU on something you can lend. Don't buy an extra pot or coffee machine; borrow it, and let your neighbor use your fax machine. However, you should never borrow without expecting to return the favor.

Negotiating

As a literary agent, I make my living negotiating, so I'm never embarrassed to say that I don't think something is priced fairly. However, I find many of my friends feel ripped off because they don't even try to negotiate for services and find out after the fact that someone else got the same service cheaper.

Just about everything is negotiable, from wedding receptions to kids' parties. Most of the time, all you have to do is ask, and the salesperson will tell you the ways in which you can cut back on the price (have the party on Friday night instead of Saturday, pay cash, book early).

Negotiating takes a little preparation. You need to make some calls so you know the going rate, and you also need to set a fairly firm budget in your head.

My company recently held a catered cocktail party for 120 people, where we decided to feature cold food, which is cheaper (see chapter 4 on catering). In the first round of calls we made to inquire about price per person for cold cuts and dips we were told $7 or $8 per person, which was close to outrageous. When we asked how we could cut the cost, a handful of caterers said we couldn't, but most offered to simplify the menu (just roast beef and turkey with two cheeses) or suggested serving a large sandwich, and we were able to cut the cost in half.

I can't tell you the number of times I've received a "firm" price from a caterer but found that after I said a competitor would charge less, there was suddenly an amazing amount of flexibility in what could be offered. This happened in the case of a midtown Manhattan hotel reception with steak and an open bar as well as a child's christening reception. Caution: make sure at the outset that there won't be any extra charges for setting up, delivery, rolls, salads, etc. All of this should be gone over in the preliminary negotiations.

Yard Sales, Flea Markets, and More

Yard sales, flea markets, rummage sales, swap meets, thrift shops, and garage sales are a gold mine for those who entertain frequently. You can often pick up extra household items at a fraction of their cost.

You would be surprised how many people don't know where to look for these sales. Most people forget that the local paper is an excellent source of information: it will list most church and institutional sales by date, as well as announce tag, estate, and, sometimes, yard sales. People also forget that the local thrift shop or Salvation Army store is a treasure trove, and you can usually find them listed in the phone book.

When I first started visiting sales, I was constantly overwhelmed by all the fabulous junk that was offered. I would either buy too much, and then not be able to use it, or regret that I hadn't bought those beautiful green goblets because I was being cheap that week. To eliminate these sources of remorse I have begun to keep a wish list of things to look for at these sales in my wallet. I take out my list before I enter. I update my wish list—a kind of entertaining inventory—on a regular basis. I know what I don't need, so I won't be liable to buy another coaster set or salt-and-pepper shaker when I already have too many.

Below is a very basic list of items I look for at flea markets:

Table linen	Candlesticks
Silver serving pieces	Pitchers
Trivets	Coasters
Large bowls (crystal is nice)	Crystal or silver salt and
Glass sets of eight or twelve	pepper shakers
(can be used for dessert)	Fancy china pieces
Chaffing dishes	(Lenox, Wedgwood, etc.)

If you don't have the basics, flea markets are a good place to buy the following:

Stack tables	Juicer
Crock pot	Small food processor
Serving trays	Hors d'oeuvre trays
Silver tea set	Punch bowl and cups

I often go straight to the person who has organized the sale and ask if they have the items I'm looking for. Often they do, but they haven't put them out. You can also ask the local thrift store to keep an eye out for a certain item for you and give them your phone number.

Using Creativity

Details make all the difference in truly memorable entertaining. It is not how much you spend on a party, but how you make use of what you spend. If you have the time, you can probably think your way out of any bind you might come up with by using creativity, and remembering that great entertaining is always in the details.

My rule of thumb on this is to choose one or two details and really go whole hog. For instance, a typical potluck dinner might feature the basic pasta salads, bean salads, and chili dishes, but you can dress the whole thing up by ordering platters of large shrimp with cocktail sauce as an extravagant appetizer.

Some of the best parties I've ever been to have probably not cost a lot to throw, but the hostess put an enormous amount of time and creativity into them. For example, one mom put together an Alice in Wonderland Mad Tea birthday party for her seven-year-old daughter and made all the decorations herself (copying the famous Tenniell illustrations onto napkins and tablecloths). She also made up games that went with the theme and then gave out miniature tea sets as party favors.

Some of the best adult parties I've ever been to have been the ones where I've had to bring my own booze. At one memorable party I had to put my share into a kitty that went for a pair of Broadway tickets for the winner of a treasure hunt. One hostess called to ask each guest to make his or her very best dish for eight—what a scrumptious meal!—and she supplied an exquisite table setting and expensive wine. A cocktail party where we were served martinis and macadamia nuts stands out in my memory as well.

Details are best when they're homemade (and cheaper that way too). You can make just about anything you might need from scratch, from appetizers to cakes, linens, and decorations. If you need help, the best place to go is the Internet. Use your favorite search engine and type in one or two words that will describe what you're looking for, such as "Thanksgiving recipes" or "birthday parties."

You can also go to the library for books on holiday and party decorating or get back issues of some of the more creative women's magazines for recipes and arts and crafts ideas.

Taking the time to come up with one or two creative details for your party will ensure that the event is remembered and will make your guests feel that you went out of your way for them.

3

Party Basics at Home

Home entertaining is a lot of fun if you are comfortable with your home. I find home creates a much more relaxed ambiance than hiring a hall and caterer or even going out to a restaurant with a group. However, it is also a lot more complicated.

One of the most important elements of home entertaining is making your guests feel welcome and that you are enjoying their company. You can't do that if you are loading the dishwasher or making a complicated glaze. You have to make a real effort to organize your meal in such a way that there is always time to talk to your guests. This is one instance where the planning of the meal, and the cleanup in between courses, is vitally important. Without adequate planning you'll spend your whole party running from the kitchen to the dinning room without ever finishing a sentence.

Whether you're having just another couple or sixty people (probably the maximum for home entertaining with comfort), you'll have to make a few decisions at the outset.

Preparing for Company

You should set aside the day before the party (or the nights after work) to make the house as spotless as possible. If you've always been meaning to clean fingerprints off the woodwork, this is the time to do it. Even if your guests don't notice it, you will during the entire party. Same goes for stains on the rug, which can easily be removed with one of those commercial rug cleaners you should have clipped coupons for.

If you have anything it would kill you to see damaged or broken, put it away, because accidents always happen. When I had my brother's going-away party, I moved all my living room furniture into the bedroom so that the guests could dance. One of the guests had too much to drink, went to lie down in the bedroom, missed the bed, and fell on my antique mahogany coffee table and broke it. One of my guests at a New Year' Eve party threw a glass from my new crystal set against the wall to ring in the new year. If children are coming, assume that they will get into everything and move your Lladró and Wedgwood out of their reach or into the china cabinet. There's nothing more difficult than trying to assure your guests that the sculpture your husband made of you on your honeymoon can be glued back together or that your Hummel collection can be easily replaced. It ruins the party for everyone.

The best thing to do is to prepare for children, putting out little dishes of popcorn, chocolate kisses, and M&Ms, things they *can* get into easily. These goodies should keep them away from the caviar and paté, which they probably won't like. Some adults will go for this stuff too.

I also warn my child that other kids are coming. I tell him to put away the toys that he does not want to share or that he would be upset about if they broke.

Put away the things you do not want your guests to become preoccupied with. I have an aunt who keeps her wedding album under the glass of her coffee table. She always complains that people who come to her house look through it and comment on how thin she was years ago. That wouldn't happen if the wedding album was out of public view.

The same thing applies to anything you don't want to share with your company. I have an uncle who collects fifty-year-old Metaxa and is upset when someone comes to his home and drinks it (one guest *did* drink an entire bottle). If it wasn't displayed prominently in his liquor cabinet, no one would know it was there.

If you are going to let people smoke, make sure there are plenty of ashtrays (if you don't have any or you don't have enough, you can pick them up at a dollar store). Otherwise state your smoking policy to guests who smoke: "smoking is permitted on the terrace" or "in the backyard."

If you're going to be using special dishes or grandmother's china, wash all the dishes and glasses the night before the party (you can check for chips this way too). If you're going to use silver, make sure it is polished ahead of time. This is not the sort of thing you should be doing as the food is cooking.

Planning the Party

If you're having less than ten people it's probably easier to invite them over the phone. For any more than that, however, you should send out invitations. How fancy or informal they are is up to you, and the occasion, if any, you are celebrating.

Many of the group dinner-party invitations I've received have been whimsical Xeroxes often including directions to the house. Since so many people have computers with laser printers, homemade computer-generated invitations are becoming more and more popular. If you don't have a computer, you might be able to find a friend, neighbor, or coworker who would make them up for you, but you will have to invite them to the party.

There are also some wonderful computer graphics programs for making invitations and cards, which you can pick up at your wholesale club for $30. This is an especially good idea if you entertain a lot and like to make computer graphics.

If two weeks have gone by and people have not RSVP'd, feel free to call. You have to know how many are coming, and people often forget the deadline you've set on the invitation.

Planning the Meal

The kind of party and food I serve depends on how many people are coming. As I said, my dining table comfortably seats twelve, and I can put up to four kids in the nearby kitchen (I believe in a kids' table), so sixteen is the maximum for a sit-down dinner in my house. You should calculate the comfortable maximum in your own home, and either borrow tables to seat more or serve dinner as a buffet, which is what I recommend once the guest list climbs above sixteen.

If I'm serving a sit-down dinner, I always serve a roast. I do these well, and my guests all seem to love them. Roasts are easy to cook and relatively inexpensive. Turkey runs between 39 and 69 cents a pound, roast beef about $1.50, so I can usually feed ten people for $10. Leg of lamb is about $1.69 per pound, so I can feed sixteen for about $30. Since a roast just needs to be seasoned and then popped in the oven for a few hours, with occasional basting, I'm left with plenty of time to work on the side dishes and appetizers.

When I shop, I am always on the lookout for a well-priced piece of meat, because I entertain about once a month. There's usually a turkey in my freezer and I will always buy a leg of lamb if it's on sale. Roast pork and ham are favorites as well. However, if you haven't bought a roast ahead of time, you can always go to a wholesale club and buy a roast at a good price.

In the summer, it is easy to vary the menu with a sumptuous seafood pasta meal, such as grilled tuna in olive oil and garlic or a shrimp scampi over pasta. A paella works well, too.

I like soups in the summer, as well. A cold gazpacho or a light egg and lemon soup is a nice way to start a meal.

Since so many people are vegetarians today, I make at least four side dishes—usually mashed potatoes (a five-pound bag of potatoes is 99 cents), a lettuce and tomato salad with vinaigrette dressing, steamed broccoli with a lemon butter sauce, and some kind of cold nosh like stuffed celery or an olive and cheese platter.

If I have the time, I might also make some kind of casserole side dish. I'm part Greek, so I like to make a pastichio (a Greek lasagna) without meat or buy a frozen pack of cheese or spinach pies (about $5 for twelve). This is quite inexpensive and definitely rounds out a meal if you have some guests who don't eat meat or who just don't like pork or lamb.

Homemade hummus and guacamole are great appetizers, and both are easy and fairly inexpensive to make. Sometimes I serve cheese or spinach pies as appetizers and later bring the leftovers to the table when dinner is served. When I'm trying to impress, I'll make stuffed mushrooms, which are inexpensive (99 cents for the mushrooms, plus bread crumbs, Parmesan cheese, and butter) but fairly time-consuming to prepare. I might also dress up deviled eggs with a topping of caviar or smoked bacon bits.

Dessert, which I make the night before the party, is usually a pie, with vanilla ice cream or homemade whipped cream. I find pies incredibly easy to make and they are always well received. If you prefer not to make your own crust, frozen pie crust works just fine. (The supermarket brands are usually the least expensive, and I've never been able to taste the difference.) Occasionally, I make walnut brownies (from a mix) or cookies.

I always put a pitcher of cold water on the dinner table, so I set my table with two glasses—one for water, one for something else. I always buy two-liter bottles of cola, a caffeine-free soda, and a diet soda, so I have a variety of drinks to offer my guests. I only buy name brands, which I can usually get for 99 cents, because I don't want to announce to my guests that I'm a cheapskate. Besides, I find on these items, I often *can* taste the difference and so, I imagine, would my guests.

For alcoholic beverages, I usually just offer wine or beer. We are not hard liquor drinkers in my house, but we do keep mixed-drink basics on hand for guests. Times have definitely changed, though, and I find people rarely drink cocktails the way I remember them doing at my parents' parties.

I only serve wines and beers that I would drink myself. When I see a bottle of wine on sale at the local wholesale store or liquor store, I will try it myself and see how it holds up. This way, I can usually offer my guests a good Merlot (Walnut Crest), white Zinfandel (Beringer's) or Pinot Grigio for $5 a bottle (the wholesale clubs will sell two-liter bottles). For beer, I try to find a twelve-pack of a good national brand (Rolling Rock, Amstel Light, Sam Adams) or local brew that runs between $7.99 and $12.99.

If I know that a number of guests are nondrinkers, I may buy a three-pack of sparkling apple cider, which I've found for about $5 at my local wholesale club. However, they only seem to stock this around Thanksgiving, Christmas, and Easter. White or red grape juice (about $2 for a sixty-four-ounce bottle or can) also works well for nondrinkers, and you can spruce it up by making it a spritzer (half seltzer, half juice).

In the summer, I like to offer my guests a champagne punch or sangria, which they all seem to love and which fits easily into any party budget. However, this just doesn't seem to work on cold winter nights. I might also offer homemade lemonade or iced tea instead of soft drinks in warmer weather.

I always offer my guests coffee or tea after dinner. I keep a small jar of instant decaffeinated coffee on hand, in case one of my guests just can't take caffeine (there was a while there when all my friends were pregnant). You can also buy a small portion of decaf and brew it in a Melita, since most people prefer fresh-brewed to instant. I also keep real cream in the house for company (usually to use for the whipped cream for dessert), which is a nice touch. Of course, I offer 2 percent milk as well.

Once you've planned the menu, you have to plan the shopping. I get whatever I can—the meat, beverages, some vegetables (potatoes, apples for a pie), and any frozen foods—way ahead of time, usually when I do my weekly shopping. Anything I have to get fresh, such as cream and salad fixings, I buy the morning of the party, after reviewing my menu the night before.

Setting the Table

Part of setting the table is planning the layout of the food and the flow of guests. Once you know how many people are coming, you know whether you are having a sit-down dinner or a buffet.

I usually have two stack tables on either side of the main couch, where I place my appetizers. If you have a coffee table, this is a good location for your hors d'oeuvres as well.

If I am having the full number of guests I can accommodate for dinner (which is sixteen for my table), I will also put a stack table near the dining table for extra beverages and ice (so I don't have to get up ten times) and perhaps the salad, after everyone has been served (this leaves more space on the table).

If you don't have stack tables, don't go out and buy them. Unless you live in the wilderness, you can certainly borrow them from a neighbor. People over fifty believed religiously in stack tables, so if you have friends of this generation (or parents or in-laws nearby), you're probably in luck. If you find they're very useful after borrowing a set a couple of times, you can usually find them at garage sales.

I believe quite strongly in using some kind of tablecloth, and also in coasters and trivets, but that's only because I finally have some nice (new) furniture and I am not partial to watermarks and stains, no matter how charming or interesting their provenance.

Flea markets are great places to look for could-have-been-in-my-family lace heirlooms at a fraction of the price you would pay for them if they were new. And don't skip those famous January white sales when department stores will reduce everything just to get you back in the stores after Christmas.

If you are using more than one table, the color of your tablecloths should match, unless the holiday you're celebrating is a two-toner (red and green for Christmas, black and orange for Halloween). However, they do not have to be the same pattern or material. You can mix lace and cloth, as long as they're the same color.

Gold is a good color for tablecloths. It is rich and elegant and usually available during the white sales because people tend to go for the basics. If you have a favorite color that goes with the decor of your home, you might want to buy two or three tablecloths in that shade when they're on sale.

Coasters usually come in sets of four, so for a party of sixteen you can't be expected to have them match. However, if you entertain a lot, you might want to invest in four matching sets of silver-plated coasters (they run between $3.99 and $5.99 a set). You should be able to pick up a set any time of the year at a discount store, and you might just be able to get a set for $1.99 right after Christmas. You can also borrow them from friends if you're having a fairly fancy gathering—everyone you know probably has at least one set of these coasters.

No one expects your trivets or hot plates to match, but it's a nice touch if they do. Again, if you can pick up the silver-plated ones when you find them on sale or buy three or four matching ones when you see them at a good price, you're way ahead of the game (The Limited catalogs are good for this, because they offer their products in lots of three).

I like to have a centerpiece on my table, whether or not I am celebrating an occasion. Sometimes I just put together an assortment of candlesticks, which should match in both material (glass, silver, or brass—you can pick most of these up at a dollar store or flea market) and candle color (white and gold are good here too) or flowers (fresh or silk is fine) or a basket of fruit or bread.

If you're artistic, try making a centerpiece. There are many ideas and kits available in craft stores and magazines and through Internet sites. While I prefer store-bought or craft-fair purchases, I did make one centerpiece that would work for any table any time of the year.

Take a plain glass vase (the kind you usually get with a flower delivery), paint a simple floral design on it with acrylic paint, and tie a ribbon (try gold, pink or lavender) around the neck. It really dresses up your table. If you're like me and keep every vase you've ever received, this is an opportunity to finally make good use out of something everyone else thinks you should throw away. If not, you can pick up a vase at a yard sale or even buy one from the local florist for very little.

Cloth napkins are nice, but they're an extravagance, especially if they're white. If you're serving red wine or any kind of red sauce or one of your guests wears the new lipstick that promises never to come off (except on your napkins), you're safer with paper. I recommend fancy white paper table napkins, which you can get at a dollar store or in lots of 300 at a wholesale club.

Your dishes, glasses, and utensils should match. By this I mean you should try to have dishes of the same color and pattern. If you don't have service for sixteen (and can't borrow it), your best bet would be to use two complete sets of eight and alternate them at the table. If you are serving twelve, but only have service for eight and have to borrow dishes or use two different sets, you should set the table with six of each pattern. Same goes for the flatware and the glassware.

For utensils, you should never mix silver and stainless steel. Borrow one set of either to make sure that all your flatware matches.

Make sure you have the right number of pieces (don't forget salad forks and coffee spoons).You don't want to have to run back into the kitchen to wash all the forks and spoons for dessert. Don't forget the serving utensils (salad servers, large spoons for the mashed potatoes, gravy spoon, pie server, ladle).

Glasses should also match, and you shouldn't mix crystal and glass, if you can help it. Not only should the material of the glasses match, but the type should match as well (wine glasses, water glasses, etc.). However, the pattern or design can be different, if it's not too obvious or if their difference is the point.

I find that sets of glasses (usually twelve to a box, with four water, four rocks, and four juice glasses) are sold in every discount store and are very cheap. You should be able to pick up a number of boxes for under $20, especially at places like IKEA, Caldor, and Kmart. I've seen boxed sets on sale for as little as $5.00 at discount stores. For mousse-like desserts, berries with cream, or cold soups, you might want to consider balloon glasses, which you can certainly pick up at a dollar store or a flea market.

You will also need to make sure you have the right serving pieces for your company, such as platters, bread baskets, coffee pots, sugar, creamers, and salt and pepper shakers. All these items should match, that is, they should be all silver or all china. What you don't have, you should be able to borrow from friends—they probably received a lot of these items as wedding presents. If you borrow silver, part of the payback might be that you'll polish it, since the owners probably haven't used it since the day they got it.

You may also have to borrow a second coffee machine, which is preferable to serving only twelve cups of coffee at a time and making some of your guests wait for the second serving.

If you're serving two roasts, you might even have to "borrow" a neighbor's oven or microwave. I once made Thanksgiving dinner for sixteen and found I had to use my downstairs neighbor's oven for the appetizers and dessert (that was before I learned to make the dessert the night before).

When having a sit-down dinner, you can never use paper or plastic plates and flatware. If you feel the need to use them, then you should be having a buffet.

I hate running back and forth to the kitchen once my guests arrive, so I try very hard to have as much as possible done ahead of time. That's why I set up the stack tables with appetizers, and it's why I set the table before the guests arrive.

Last-Minute Preparations

Make the salad about a half an hour before the company is due and put it in the refrigerator, but do not dress it (do make the the dressing ahead of time, though). If I'm serving a plate of pickles, olives, and cheese, I prepare the dish early, cover it with plastic wrap, and put it in the fridge. Cold hors d'oeuvres (dips, guacamole, or hummus) should be prepared right before the guests are due, so that they are fresh. If appetizers need to be baked or zapped, I have them ready to go directly into the oven or microwave so that they're hot when my guests arrive. If cheese needs to be softened, it's out on the kitchen table an hour before the guests come. Put together the cracker or bread basket before the guests arrive as well.

Atmosphere

I'm not a big one for perfumed candles, aromatherapy, or incense. I believe the smell of a meal cooking or the aroma of a pie baking is more than enough to enthrall my guests. However, I feel that music is extremely important to setting the mood of the meal. Therefore, I think it's imperative that you set aside some time during the planning stage to decide about how long the party should be (usually four hours for a dinner party) and choose the music you wish to play for your company. Take a few minutes before your guests arrive to make sure the music you've chosen is all cued up.

Whether it's a sit-down dinner party or a buffet the music should be background music, although it can be a little livelier if you're having a cocktail party. The music you play for your guests should have a uniformity to it—by this I mean you should not be mixing rock with country and classical.

Since I like my parties to have a theme, I like the music to fit the theme in some way. If I'm having a Christmas dinner, I'll play Christmas music. If the meal is of a certain ethnicity, I might play music from that region. If I'm throwing a thirtieth birthday party, I might play music from the birthday guest's teenage years. You might choose to just play music from a certain decade or of a certain type (jazz, show tunes, opera, soft rock).

Before my husband and I had children, he would often spend hours making tapes to play when we entertained. Now, the best we can do is put aside a handful of CDs. However, it is important that you choose the music before your guests arrive or you will be running to and from the stereo each time a CD ends. Even worse, a guest might take it upon himself to choose the music for you, and you might then spend a good deal of the evening explaining why you own *The Best of the Partridge Family*. There are, however, a number of multi-disc players on the market. So if you have one, take advantage of the hours' worth of music it can provide.

Buffets

Most of the rules of sit-down dining apply for buffet-style at-home dining, except that you can use paper or plastic plates, utensils, flatware, and even tablecloths (which you should buy at a wholesale club or at a discount or dollar store where you might be able to pick up a pattern of some sort). Everyone understands that you are using too many dishes for the average dishwasher.

A nice touch when having a buffet is to wrap the cutlery in the napkins and tie them with a ribbon, preferably one that goes with the decor. Place them, standing up, in a basket, so that guests can just grab a setting without having to fumble for the individual pieces.

You might want to think about putting an extra wastebasket near the dining table, so that people don't have to crowd into the kitchen to throw away their dirty dishes. If you live in a state that recycles, you might want to have a separate wastebasket just for cans and bottles. This will also make it easier for people to clean up after themselves, and you won't have so many empty bottles to collect after the party.

When setting the table make sure you put out an ample number of napkins, as people will inevitably spill things, and you want them to be able to clean up as fast as possible. If there is more than one course served (appetizers, main course, dessert) you should have at least the number of courses times the number of guests in napkins (3 courses × 25 guests = 75 napkins). The same math applies for cups, because people tend to throw out empty cups and then get fresh ones when they're thirsty again.

If you are using more than one table, you should have the same items on each table, so people won't crowd around the turkey and skip the salad. Furthermore, at large gatherings, having an extra table helps spread people out and keeps the buffet line moving.

For beverages, put a punch bowl on the table or put a cooler full of ice with beer and soda in it under the table. You can also place an ice bucket on the table and display the wine, beer, and soda on one side of the table. Make sure you leave at least two bottle openers on the table if the beer or the wine require them. Always put out a pitcher of cold water for your guests too.

The food you decide to serve will depend on the number of guests you have and perhaps on the time of year (lighter food in the summer). For twenty-five people and under, I might serve a large turkey or a roast and a casserole (lasagna, ham and spaghetti casserole). If I'm having more than twenty-five, I would serve several main courses (Greek meatballs, which I can make the night before; a casserole, which I will make ahead and reheat before the party; and a roast) as well as a number of side dishes. Pasta dishes are also great for large crowds.

If you are serving a roast, you will probably need two gravy boats and at least two salt and pepper shakers.

Keep in mind, too, that finger food is the easiest thing for standing guests to eat. Gravies and sauces are likely to end up on your floor and upholstery if your guests have nowhere to sit.

Dessert can be much the same as what you would serve at a sit-down dinner, although I would probably make two to three different pies (apple, blueberry, strawberry, or banana creme) or brownies. For a buffet, homemade cookies are also a great choice.

Unless you can get your local church or PTA to lend you their coffeemaker, you are definitely going to have to borrow a second coffee machine. You should have at least two creamers and sugar bowls as well.

Many couples receive large hot plates, crockpots, and silver warming trays as wedding presents, so you should be able to borrow as many of these as you need from friends. Just make sure you don't wait until the last minute to locate these important appliances. (Sometimes your friends think they know where things are and then realize the night of your party that they threw them out.) You might want to look into borrowing stack tables to place strategically around the room as well.

Cocktail Parties

A cocktail party is any party where dinner is not served. I gave a lot of cocktail parties and was invited to a lot of them when I was younger, single, and childless.

Cocktail parties start later than dinner parties and usually end later too. During my parents' youth, they used to start early and end early so people could go out to dinner afterward, but today they tend to be after-dinner gatherings.

Some cocktail party invitations give a specific time, such as 6:00 to 8:00 P.M. This means that the party is finite, usually because there is another event to attend, such as a live performance. If the invitation just states a time to begin, such as 7:00 P.M., then the party is open-ended. I like to start a cocktail party between 7:00 and 8:00 P.M. and hope that the last guest will be on the way home no later than 1:00 A.M., but that's really up to you and your guests (and perhaps your neighbors).

Even though you're not required to feed your guests, I always have enough appetizers and finger foods available for someone to make a meal of it if they have to. I'm always worried that someone will have too much to drink on an empty stomach and drive home.

For the average cocktail party, my appetizers include lots of chips and dips. I offer homemade salsa and bowls of taco chips, as well as guacamole. Near the bowls of pretzels and potato chips (staples at this kind of thing), I place small bowls of dip. I pop a few bags of microwave popcorn and put it out in bowls. Dribble on a little melted butter, and you will be considered a party goddess. Little bowls of M&Ms, chocolate kisses, and Reeses Peanut Butter cups will disappear immediately. I have also found that people love to be offered bowls of nuts, especially something more exotic than peanuts, so I often put out a few helpings of shelled nuts like roasted almonds or pistachios. All of this, while being pretty effortless, adds up to a nice variety of nibbles.

The above items can be bought quite cheaply in bulk at your local wholesale club. The candy might even be less expensive at your supermarket, if you've managed to clip the coupons that always come out around Halloween, Valentine's Day, and Easter. (Ferrero hazelnut balls and Cadbury chocolate bars, broken into serving pieces, also make a nice touch.)

For a slightly fancier cocktail party, I would also include an assortment of cheeses, with crackers and French bread wedges. I might also offer a paté and olives and possibly a platter of smoked salmon with bread slices. You can buy a whole side of smoked salmon at a wholesale club for $14.

You might also add a fruit platter, with grapes and apple and pear slices. In the summer, you might try offering an assortment of strawberries, raspberries, and blueberries with whipped cream. I've been to parties where creative hostesses have carved out a watermelon and filled the rind with melon balls and assorted summer fruit. Fresh pineapple chunks are also well received in the summer.

If you choose to serve hot appetizers, you can buy packages of thirty-six of almost anything at your local wholesale club for about $5. This usually includes such hors d'oeuvres as miniature hot dogs, cheese puffs, egg rolls, and poppers. Most of these wholesale clubs offer shoppers a sample of this kind of fare at various times throughout the year, so you should have a pretty good idea of how these frozen foods will taste. My one rule of thumb with these appetizers is never offer something to your guests you haven't tried yourself.

In addition to the store-bought appetizers, I might offer one or two homemade items, such as Greek meatballs (which can be served hot or cold) or my reliable hummus with pita bread slices.

On the beverages front, I would do much the same as at a sit-down dinner or buffet party regarding soda, wine, and beer. However, if my cocktail party had a theme (disco, New Year's, bon voyage), I might make a pitcher or two or three of a mixed drink that I felt would go

well with the theme such as tequila sunrises or champagne punch or
piña coladas, all of which are much cheaper to make if you buy the
ingredients in large quantities. Just make sure you have a lot of ice
and enough to go around for at least three drinks per guest. You might
want to borrow an extra blender if you're throwing a frozen-drinks
party.

Setting up for a cocktail party is much like setting up for a buffet.
You place everything on the dining room table, with snack bowls
spread strategically throughout your home, as well as the extra waste-
baskets. If it's a casual cocktail party (end of the semester, office
party), you can use plastic and paper. If it's black tie (tenth wedding
anniversary), you need to go to cloth and silver, but you can use those
plastic champagne glasses.

Music is especially important at cocktail parties. If you're having a
party where you expect guests to talk to one another, you need to
have four or five hours of seamless background music picked out.

If you're having a party where you expect your guests to dance, or
at least get up and wiggle, you need to plan the music carefully. If you
don't have four or five hours of the right kind of music, you don't have
to run to the record store and buy five hours of Latin jazz. You can
borrow CDs from the local library or from friends. I recommend that
you move your living room furniture out of the way. Anything that can
break probably will, and your guests will feel less inhibited if you give
them the space they need.

A cocktail party is the one kind of party at which I've had to tell
guests it's time to go home. Most sit-down or buffet parties break up
after one or two couples leave. Changing the tone of the music to
something soft when you think it's time to wind down is one subtle
way of calling it a night. People also start to get the hint if you start
cleaning up aggressively (folding up the paper tablecloths, emptying
ashtrays). However, if none of the above works, don't be ashamed to
say the party's over by offering the last few guests their coats. Part of
the whole idea of throwing parties is for you to enjoy your company,
and for you to want to do it again. Don't let one rude guest lead you
to second thoughts.

Sample Menus

Below are sample menus and estimated costs for three parties: a sit-down dinner, a buffet party, and a cocktail party. Cost estimates are based on average prices in Eastern United States supermarkets or wholesale clubs. This should give you an idea of the kind of budgeting your party will require.

Sit-Down Dinner for 12

Hummus dip with pita bread $ 6.00

> 1 16-ounce can of chick peas, juice of 1 lemon, tahini paste, pita bread. (You will be able to use the tahini paste at least five more times, so this is actually very economical if you entertain a lot.)

Guacamole $ 4.00

> 2 ripe Haas avocados, juice of 1 lemon, 2 tablespoons chili powder, 1 garlic clove

Roast turkey—14 pounds × 69 cents per pound = $ 9.66

Garlic mashed potatoes $ .99

> 1 5-pound bag potatoes, 3 tablespoons butter, $1/4$ cup cream or milk, 1 garlic clove

Cornbread stuffing $ 1.82

> 1 $8^1/_2$-ounce box Jiffy cornbread mix, 1 small box raisins, 10 to 15 walnuts

Salad $ 3.00

> 1 head of red leaf lettuce, 2 or 3 plum tomatoes, onion, a few olives, oil and vinegar

Carrots	$ .99

1 6-ounce bag of baby carrots, 2 teaspoons sugar, 2 tablespoons butter

Apple pie	$ 3.38

6 or 7 apples (bag), pie crust

Chocolate cream pie	$ 1.68

1 box chocolate pudding mix, 5 or 6 graham crackers

Whipped cream	$ .99

1 pint heavy whipping cream, 1 tablespoon sugar

Soda, 3 2-liter bottles	$ 2.97
Wine, 3 bottles	$11.97
Total	**$47.45**

You can reduce the cost of the meal by making less expensive appetizers or serving a punch and iced tea instead of soda or wine.

When I calculate the cost of the meal, I am not counting the cost of basic staples such as sugar, butter, flour, coffee, tea that will be used in small quantities. The meal could run you as much as $10 more if you have to buy everything.

Buffet for 35

Hummus	$ 7.00

(Cost goes up about a dollar for every ten extra people you serve.)

Guacamole	$ 5.00

(Cost goes up an additional $1 to $1.50 for every ten people)

Potato chips	$ 2.59

2 pound bag

Tortilla chips	$ 2.59

2 pound bag

Onion dip with bleu cheese	$ 3.00

1 pint sour cream, 1 package onion soup mix, 1/8 pound crumbled blue cheese

Roast turkey	$ 9.66
Lasagna (2 trays homemade)	$ 9.99

1-pound boxes lasagna noodles, 1 pound ground beef, ricotta cheese, mozzarella cheese

Salad	$ 5.00
Garlic mashed potatoes	$ .99
Stuffed celery	$ 5.00

1 bunch celery stalk, 8 ounces soft cream cheese, 8 ounces blue cheese, paprika

Cornbread stuffing	$ 2.65

2 boxes of Jiffy cornbread, 2 small boxes of raisins

Apple pie	$ 3.38
Brownies (with walnuts)	$ .99
Oatmeal cookies with raisins and walnuts	$ 2.00
Whipped cream	$ .99
Soda, 5 2-liter bottles	$ 4.95
Beer (1 case)	$ 15.00
White wine, 2 bottles	$ 10.00
Red Wine, 2 bottles	$ 10.00
Ice, 5 pounds	$ 5.00
2 paper tablecloths	$ 2.00
Chinet plates	$ 5.00
Dinner napkins	$ 1.00
Plastic utensils (assorted)	$ 3.00
Plastic tumblers	$ 1.00
Total	**$117.78**

Again, the cost of the party can be greatly reduced if you offer iced tea and lemonade instead of soda, and serve a punch or eliminate the alcoholic beverages. However, even with the alcoholic drinks, this party comes to less than $3.50 per person, which is very good. Leaving out the alcohol lowers the cost to about $2.50 per person.

Fancy Cocktail Party for 50

Hummus	$ 9.00
Guacamole	$ 7.00
Potato chips	$ 2.59
Tortilla chips	$ 2.59
Salsa	$ 5.00
homemade or store-bought	
Pretzels	$ 2.00
Candy	$ 3.00
assorted	
Cheese	$ 15.00
assorted—Brie with almonds, Saga bleu, cheddar	
Bread	$ 3.00
2 loaves of Italian or French, cut in wedges	
Carr's crackers, 4 boxes	$ 4.49
Olives	$ 7.00
3 pounds assorted; Spanish, Greek	
Paté	$ 5.00
2-pound package	
Greek meatballs	$ 7.00
5 pounds of ground beef or lamb makes about sixty meatballs	
Pasta salad	$ 7.00
3 pounds macaroni with dressing and peas and ham	

Soda, 9 bottles assorted, including seltzer	$ 9.99
2 cases of beer	$ 30.00
Wine	$ 30.00
3 1-liter bottles or 2 jugs each of white and red	
Ice, plates, etc., about the same as above	$ 20.00
Carrot cake for 50	$ 15.99
Total	**$185.65**

Once again, you can reduce the cost of the party by making a punch and iced tea and lemonade. You might want to try a sangria or pitchers of drinks for this kind of party, instead of the beer and wine, which accounts for about one-third of the party's cost. You can also replace the Greek meatballs and pasta salad with $15.00 worth of store-bought, ready-made hors d'oeuvres (which should be about 150 individual pieces), if you don't have the time to make everything.

This party comes to a little over $3.50 a head, which is still a good deal. Aside from cutting back on the alcohol, you can lower the price per person by making your own dessert or cutting out some of the food. There's a lot of food here!

4

Catered Parties

If you are having more than sixty people, or if you just don't want to do all the cleaning, shopping, schlepping, and setting up yourself, you might want to consider having your party catered.

Catering might sound expensive, but there are many different ways to do it. It all depends on what you want and what you can afford. However, catering will always cost more than doing everything yourself.

The three basic categories of catering are: in your home, in rented space, or in a restaurant. Of course, the more you have someone else do for you (such as setting up and cleaning up), the more expensive it will be.

Catering in Your Home

The first catered party I had was my parents' twenty-fifth wedding anniversary (I was twenty-four). My aunt knew a woman in her neighborhood who supplemented her Social Security checks by cooking and baking from home, so we were able to get a good price on homemade food. This is actually a wonderful way to cater a party, if you know someone who is a good cook and might like to earn some extra money. This is an especially good idea if you are looking for a particular ethnic favorite. Someone who has been making a specialty for years will do a much better job than a generic caterer.

You can inquire at your local house of worship if there is a member of the congregation who might be interested in making extra money this way. It doesn't even have to be your church or synagogue. You can just call the parish house and ask to speak with the secretary. They usually know everything and everybody. Some of the retired older women might be quite interested in baking you a cake or making a lasagna or two. If there is a senior center near you, you might call there as well. Check the classified ads in the local newspaper too.

We catered the hot food and the dessert, which was a black forest cake (something I would never attempt from scratch) and the rest we did ourselves, which included the family favorites. For drinks we served only my parents' two favorite alcoholic beverages—champagne cocktails for my mom and Manhattans for my dad—on trays in plastic champagne glasses or drink glasses, and that was a big hit.

There were thirty-five people and the party came to about $100, which was a lot for me at the time. However, I could never have afforded to take these people to a restaurant on my meager salary, and they all had a fairly luxurious evening without breaking my bank account. A party like this would run me about $250 today.

I have since had many a catered party in my home (or a borrowed home) from the assorted cold-cut-platter-and-sheet-cake setup to the shrimp cocktail and lasagna/meatballs/chicken dish affair. As with all parties, the first thing to do is set a budget and see what you can get for the price. You have to decide which is more important or where your flexibility is—time or money.

For me, if I've decided to have some of the party catered, it's because I know I don't have the time to get everything ready myself. However, there is some mystical point of being overcharged where I will decide I'll get up at six in the morning and do it myself rather than get ripped off. Only you know where that point is.

If you are going for the dip-and-veggies platter, assorted cold cuts and sheet cake, I strongly recommend that you order everything from your local wholesale club (call ahead of time). It will be much cheaper than the supermarket deli or local caterer. It will be almost as cheap as buying everything in bulk and setting it up yourself. The one drawback is that *you* (or a family member or someone who loves you very much) will have to pick up everything the day of the party.

The other advantage to this is that you, not the caterer, get to decide how much food you need. Every party I've ever had done by a catering business left me with so much extra food that I had to force it into the hands of departing guests. In one instance I gave pounds of leftover cold cuts to a homeless shelter. If you can see the food ahead of time, you'll have a much better idea of how many people a platter will feed.

For the average affair of crudites with dip, cold cuts and a sheet cake, you should expect one cold-cut platter to feed twenty people ($22.99 per five-pound platter) and each veggie-and-dip platter to feed twenty for $16.99. The sheet cake will run $24 to feed sixty, so the basic cost of this kind of party is about $2.50 per person, without drinks, and any extras you might want to throw in (like a tub of hummus, a salad, that side of salmon).

If you hire a caterer, remember the caterer always errs on the side of abundance, so if you say you need food for fifty people, expect enough to feed seventy-five. If you're having fifty people, tell the caterer thirty-five. You'll still have more than enough food.

Always comparison shop with caterers. I do this over the phone and ask them to fax me their menus and prices. There can be tremendous price discrepancies. If you like one place much better than the other, but the other is a lot cheaper, you can always quote the other's price to try to get the one you like to meet it. Most caterers will. They don't want to lose the business.

New York City caterers (which are the ones I deal with) charge between $5 and $8 per person for a cold-cut platter (with assorted bread) and veggies with dip. The sheet cake is extra (about a dollar per person), although the classier the establishment, the fancier the cake selection. Most caterers give you plates, utensils, and napkins with your order.

However, a caterer will also charge you tax, which could be a substantial amount, and you have to tip the guys who deliver the food to you (between $10 and $25, depending on how much you order). Sometimes (especially in New York) they even charge you for delivery.

You can always negotiate with the caterer. You can keep the cost of the cold cuts down by limiting your selection to, say, turkey and roast beef with American and Provolone cheese. (*Hint:* always order *smoked* turkey; it stays fresh longer than baked turkey so you can eat it longer if you overorder.) You should always tell the caterer the price is a little more than you expected, even if it's not, and ask how you can keep the price down.

The giant hero sandwich (in either the Italian or classic combination) is also a good way to cater a party and keep the cost down. These run between $5 and $10 per foot, which feeds somewhere between four and six people, and are usually supplemented by vats of cole slaw, potato salad, or macaroni salad, or even a regular salad.

It is not much more expensive to cater hot food for your guests. The lasagna/meatballs/chicken dish setups usually run about $7 to $10 per person. The caterer usually throws in a salad of some sort with this, as well as the plate, utensil, and napkin setup. The chafing dishes and sternos should be included in this price, but some caterers might ask for a refundable deposit on each item.

A more luxurious party could even feature a roast (turkey will run between $25 and $50, depending on the size) or fancier meals like chicken parmigiana or shrimp scampi, but once you go in that direction, the catering charge per person usually climbs into double digits. To my mind, you might as well go to a restaurant, where they cook it, serve it, and clean it up afterward. If you're a good negotiator, you can probably find a restaurant that will serve your party for about the same cost as doing this at home.

Renting Space for a Catered Party

If you know you can't, or don't want to, have the party in your home, there are a number of options, most of which depend on how fancy the party is and how much money you have to spend.

When I'm faced with these circumstances, my first thought is *Can I borrow someone's house? Is there some space I can use that I don't have to pay for?* I borrowed my aunt's apartment for my parents' twenty-fifth anniversary, I used my office for my husband's surprise thirtieth party, and I had a small party for my son's christening at the church where he was baptized. A friend hosted her nephew's summer birthday party in the local park, where she could use the outdoor picnic tables.

Of course, if you borrow someone else's home, you have to invite them to the party, and you have to offer to give them the lion's share of the leftovers. You also have to offer either your own home in exchange (if it's a good friend's house and they're hosting your spouse's surprise birthday party for you) or your help when they have a party and need a hand.

You should not ask to "borrow" a home from someone you do not consider a close friend or colleague (if you borrow the office). You also have to be responsible for all cleaning up, and you have to replace anything that gets ruined or broken. If the rug gets badly stained, you have to be willing to pay for it to be cleaned. In some ways, it's just easier to rent space, although more and more churches and co-op boards are asking for a refundable security deposit in case something breaks or is stained.

The most likely rental spaces are church rec rooms and party rooms in apartment building co-ops. Social organizations such as the local Y, the Kiwanis Club, Veteran's organizations, the American Legion, and some municipal buildings in small towns also rent space. Check your local phone directory for listings under "caterers," as well as the local paper.

Most of these facilities have a kitchen off of the main room, where you can store items in the refrigerator or heat things up in the oven or microwave. They also usually have extra tables and chairs and coat racks for you to use in setting up your party (these items are pricey to rent if your space doesn't provide them). Sometimes they even have a dance floor.

Renting a rec room or party room usually runs between $35 and $100, and you might be asked to write an additional check for a refundable security deposit.

Every space you rent will have its own set of rules and regulations. Most churches do not allow you to serve alcohol on their premises. Some places don't want you to play loud music. Some buildings only stay open until a certain time.

If you decide to use a rented space, you have to be very careful in planning your affair. Don't assume that you can set up the party the night before (if you're having a luncheon) because the space may be in use then. If you store your nonperishables (plates and soda) in the kitchen before the party, there's always the possibility that some-one might not know whose stuff it is and some, or all, of it may be missing when you show up to set up for your party. This caution also applies to leaving leftovers in the refrigerator until the next day after the party: they might not be there when you return.

Almost any building or institution in a major city can be rented for the right price for a private party. I know a couple who rented out the Central Park Zoo for their child's first birthday (it ran them about $6,000). Old homes that have been turned into museums are often used for this purpose. Most of these sites are quite expensive to rent, but they are sometimes free or rented at cost to an employee. If you work for a private university, they usually have property that you might be able to rent for a fraction of what they would charge an outsider. Professional clubs (alumni, sports, work-related) often also have a wonderful space that they make available to members.

If you are renting space and having the food delivered by a sepa-rate caterer, the caterer will not set it up for you unless you negotiate this. You'll have to negotiate a time to go to the premises and arrange where the food and beverages will be placed. I would recommend you do this an hour or so before the party, especially if you're planning to prepare some of the food right before the party, such as a punch.

If the party is for a special occasion, and you have decorations and balloons, you'll have to put these up yourself before the party. Make sure the hall shows you where the ladder is. Expect to bring your own staple gun and scotch tape. Don't forget aluminum foil and plastic bags or Tupperware for leftovers.

Hosting Your Party in a Restaurant

Throwing your party in a restaurant is the most expensive way to entertain, but it's also the least amount of work—no setting up, no serving, no cleaning up.

Just because you've decided to take the path of least exertion doesn't mean you have to blindly hand over your credit card. Every-thing can be negotiated, even if you're having a wedding reception at the Waldorf Astoria (*especially* if you're having a wedding reception at the Waldorf).

If I am going to have my party in a restaurant, I want the intimacy of serving in my home with the comfort of not having to cook and serve, so I look for a place that has a private room or section for my party, whether it's for twelve or thirty-five. Otherwise, you might as well have a few friends meet in a restaurant while people you don't know ogle your birthday cake and presents (I have been to parties like this, and they're a little too casual for my taste).

Friday and Saturday nights are premium evenings, so if you can schedule your party on a Sunday or a weeknight, you should be able to save money. Most restaurants will charge less if you fill the place on Monday night than if you take up the back room on the busiest nights.

If you do have some date and time flexibility, try having a luncheon, brunch, or even breakfast instead of a dinner. The earlier the meal, the cheaper the price. If the restaurant offers an early-bird special to its regular customers, you can ask if they will give you an early-bird special price for your group affair. Also, people are less inclined to drink alcohol earlier in the day, so there's usually a savings in that area as well.

Different types of meals are also priced differently in most restaurants. The chicken and pasta meals are the least expensive, followed by fish, and then beef. If you are having children attend the meal, it is important that the restaurant of your choice have a children's menu with the reduced prices that most children's menus feature.

You will have to be comfortable with asking for ways to reduce the price of the meal per person, and you will have to do it many times to get the best price ("What if I have the party another night?" "What if I only offered chicken and pasta dishes?" "Do you have a children's menu?"). If you don't ask, the restaurant will not offer the information.

Of course, you can keep the cost of the meal down by not offering appetizers or just offering your guests the house salad with the meal. The restaurant might offer pitchers of soda and iced tea instead of individual glasses, if you ask.

Another way to keep costs down is to bring your own wine or champagne. Be prepared to be charged a corking fee, which is still substantially less than what you might have to pay if the restaurant supplied the wine. If you are going to offer more of a liquor selection, you could ask for a price on pitchers of margaritas, Bloody Marys, mimosas, and beer.

If you want something really special for dessert, or a family member makes a special treat, you might consider bringing your own dessert, which will certainly cost less than the restaurant's dessert menu. You can also threaten to bring in your own dessert, which might make the restaurant give you a break on this feature of the meal.

Remember that on top of the price per meal, you will have to pay tax and a gratuity, which is often as high as 20 percent for large parties.

Having an affair catered is supposed to make your life easier so that you can more fully enjoy the company of your guests and the special event that has brought you all together.

5

Special Occasion Parties

Most of the parties I throw are for special occasions, such as birthdays and holidays. Most people have a basic party (see chapter 3) that they know how to do well and that they dress up for that special occasion, but it is the details of each gathering, even if you have the same people for the same reasons every year, that will make each party stand out.

I know that I will throw at least twenty-five gatherings and parties a year (four birthday parties, Thanksgiving, a number of Christmas get-togethers, Easter, New Year's, summer barbecues, as well as sit-down dinners for friends and family), so I'm always on the lookout for decorations that will enhance the gathering at various times of the year.

I have a large box of Christmas stuff that includes the usual bulbs and nativity, but also includes tablecloths, a set of Christmas dishes, platters, and a ceramic Santa cookie jar, which I often use as a center-piece. When my family and friends come for the annual holiday gatherings, my house is totally decked out in Christmas decor. Most of this stuff I've picked up for half price or better the day after Christmas (all major department stores have an after-Christmas sale) or at a dollar store or discount shop. I once bought a ten-piece Dickens porcelain village for $5 over Labor Day, and it's now one of our family heirlooms.

I've done the same thing for Halloween, which is a big deal in our home (my husband and son call me the queen of Halloween). We have another box in storage that is bursting with Halloween tablecloths, salt and pepper shakers, pot holders, and decorative table centerpieces.

I also have a lot of nice things for Thanksgiving and Easter, since I'm the one who always hosts those holidays, although many of those accessories are more generically seasonal, fall or spring, so I can use them for a longer period of time. It's wonderful to know I don't have to go searching for tablecloths and centerpieces the day before the holiday.

I have a neighbor who is the favorite aunt to a number of children of all ages. She often finds herself throwing a makeshift party for a group of ten to twelve kids, and she is always prepared. Always have a fresh supply of birthday cake candles on hand, which you can buy for a dollar or less a box. Many of the holiday centerpieces I've picked up over the years are ceramic, and you might find (or make) one that has a birthday motif. The same goes for a tablecloth.

However, there are some parties that call for unique and creative approaches, such as showers and retirement bashes. These occasions come so rarely in our lives, that we really want to make them as special as possible, without going broke.

Baby and Bridal Showers

No woman alive has escaped forced attendance at showers, many of which are so uninspired they can scarcely be called parties. Some of these showers have also been amazingly expensive, just because the person throwing it was too lazy to do anything creative. But baby and bridal showers are two kinds of parties where you can really go crazy with all that cute feminine stuff that women usually keep under control, because even if the men are invited, they rarely show up.

When I got married, I was running a local newspaper and was in the process of getting sued, so I was not very into the *ooh*'s and *aah*'s of being the bride. I told my mother and matron of honor that I didn't want a bridal shower, but I'm glad they didn't listen to me. So this is the first rule here: no matter what the bride says, throw her a shower.

If she's really against it and is hardly even having a wedding (the old justice of the peace routine at City Hall), throw her an anti-shower (make everyone wear black, get black balloons, spray-paint some silk flowers black, etc.), but do *something* to commemorate the event. Even if it's her third or seventh trip down the aisle (and you've thrown all the other showers), do it once more.

Remember that the purpose of these showers is to have a great time with friends on the cusp of this new life change, and to endow the bride or mother-to-be with as much stuff as possible for her new life. Where you have the shower, what you serve, how fancy the invitations are, don't really matter. What the bride or Mom gets is the key.

Invitations to showers can be store-bought or homemade (a postcard collage from back issues of *Brides* magazine or *Parents,* which you should be able to pick up for free if you ask the local library for their oldest issues) or even photocopied. I received a homemade invitation to a baby shower in the shape of a cloth diaper, with a safety pin secured into it. It was precious and memorable.

Remember to include directions because people will be coming from many different places for this gathering. Also, don't forget to put the RSVP phone number and date to respond by on the invitation.

I have always disliked having a list of the bride's colors or what to get the bride included with my invitation. If you feel you must, a discreet line about where the bride is registered is all that's needed. Same thing goes for a baby registry.

Most bridal showers are thrown by the maid of honor or the bridal party, but a beloved aunt or favorite cousin can take on the task. This usually happens when the wedding party has to come in from out of town. Sometimes, the bride gets two showers this way—one for family and one for friends and coworkers.

My experience is that showers tend to be on weekend afternoons. I guess that this is because the guys can go off to do something else (like watch a ballgame or play golf) without being left home alone. An office shower is often during lunch or right after work.

I have been to extremely fancy showers in expensive restaurants where I hardly knew what silverware to use, and one in which I was asked to bring $10 toward the purchase of the mother-to-be's gift as well as a contribution to the potluck luncheon. The latter, by the way, was one of the best showers I've ever been to, because it really made me feel like I was part of an intimate group celebrating something special.

Since showers tend to be in the afternoon, the food is generally lunch or finger food that can double as lunch. This usually means cold-cut platters or a big sandwich with an assortment of hot or cold appetizers (lots of veggies and dip) or sandwiches of chicken and tuna salad. Mixed drinks are rarely served (although a pitcher of margaritas should certainly loosen up any group of celebrants). Most showers feature soft drinks, wine, and perhaps a punch.

Cake is very important to a shower, and you should put some effort into being creative with this menu item, if you can. This can be as simple as asking the store's cake decorator if she has any additional decorations she can put on or draw on. Alternatively, you might consider doing some decorating yourself (interconnecting wedding rings or a stork carrying a baby). Go to a toy, dollar, or party store, or check out a catalog, and see if you can find some miniature furniture or dolls that you can plant into the icing. If you're truly gifted with cake decorating or are extremely artistic, you might even want to bake your own cake, cut it into an interesting shape (such as a cradle or bells), and decorate it yourself.

There should be an element of fun to the shower, and this can be kicked off by having a "wishing well" or umbrella full of small gifts for the bride or mother-to-be. Party stores will rent these (the cost is minimal, around $10, with a deposit of $25 or $35). For my bridal shower, my best friend bought a white wicker hamper, tied a big ribbon around it, and had the guests bring an inexpensive household gift, such as dish towels, pot holders, and wine openers. I've been to baby showers where we've been asked to do the same thing, with guests bringing bottles, pacifiers, and rattles. All of these items can be purchased at a dollar store.

Never feel pressured into overspending for the bigger present. If you're pressed for cash, you can call the mother of the bride or mother-to-be (or the person who is throwing the party) and ask if you can contribute to a bigger present. Often, friends and family members go in together to get some big-ticket items such as luggage or strollers. Whatever you give toward this item should be appreciated.

However, if that doesn't feel right, the other thing you can do is make something (or ask someone you know to make something) for the bride or the baby. Some of my most treasured gifts were the hand-made sweaters and booties for my son or the homemade quilts. One older woman from my mother's church made me a collage of my son's birth, which I love (she took a deep frame and glued a minia-ture crib, birth certificate, etc., into it to create a baby's room). Another woman gave me a sculpture spelling out my son's name in children's alphabet blocks.

If you're a family member and have old wedding pictures from either his or her family or baby pictures, you could have these printed and put together as a very personal photo album for the bride or new mother.

If you're throwing the shower or you're part of an important group at this shower (one of the four aunts, her sorority sisters, etc.) and you're somewhat good at sewing, you could suggest that a number of guests get together and make a quilt or embroider a tablecloth with matching napkins (just about every woman knows how to do the cross-stitch). This kind of gift is priceless and will become a family heirloom.

After the gifts have been opened, you might want to make a bonnet out of the bows and ribbons from the presents (use a paper plate as the headpiece, staples, and ribbons to tie the hat on). It's lots of fun and makes for silly pictures.

If you want to give out souvenirs, you do not have to go through a party store or wedding planner. Many Greek or Italian family events feature Jordan almonds wrapped in tulle and tied with a commemo-rative ribbon (John and Sally, Feb. 14, 1998). You can buy the Jordan almonds at the supermarket or a wholesale club, the tulle by the yard, and just pay to have the ribbon printed. This should keep the memento's cost to less than a dollar per person.

You can also go to your local dollar store, where you should be able to find beautiful mementos appropriate for a wedding (vases, candle holders, small boxes, many of which have angels or flowers on them) or a baby's birth (all manner of ceramic items such as blue or pink booties, teddy bears, bottles).

Bachelor/Bachelorette Parties

These parties usually take place the night before or the weekend before the wedding. They are usually the responsibility of the best man or the maid/matron of honor, although a sibling is often corralled into helping at the last minute. The bridal party is expected to share the cost and planning of these parties, but often doesn't.

Therefore, it is also true that bachelor and bachelorette parties can be very expensive and extremely humiliating. Too many bad movies have given many people unreal expectations of what kind of party this should be, and those hosting one are often inexperienced at throwing a party to begin with.

These parties should be well planned because there is usually a lot of drinking, and they can often last until the wee hours of the morning. Whoever hosts a bachelor party should make sure that the guests have eaten dinner, because drinking on an empty stomach can be dangerous, especially if guests are driving.

A few bachelorette parties I've attended started after dinner (around 8:00 or 9:00 P.M.), but I would suggest an earlier start so that food is involved, and perhaps you'll have an earlier evening overall (especially if the wedding is the next day). Even if you are planning on going out on the town later on, I would suggest an easy-to-prepare meal of lasagna, salad, and garlic bread (homemade or ordered from the local deli).

Invitations to this kind of party are usually made by phone or word of mouth. Most bachelorette parties consist of the bridal party, a few female family members who must be invited (such as the groom's sister-in-law), and the bride's best friends, so it's usually not more than twenty-five people, and often somewhere between eight and sixteen.

The most popular way to throw a bachelor party is to do it in a restaurant or bar. Men tend to rent out back rooms, which can be outrageously expensive (I'd rather just give the couple the cash) or meet at places like Hooters or go bar-hopping to strip clubs. Women tend to go to a favorite restaurant, club, or perhaps a Chippendale's-like establishment. This kind of evening can run each participant $100 (because you *always* treat the groom- or bride-to-be) and, if only one or two people are paying, this kind of party can run a tab of something like $1,000. Many bridal parties are shell-shocked by the cost of the night before party.

When my husband was recently tapped for best-man service, he called around to see how much dinner at a men's club would be for the guys and quickly decided that the $700 tab was just too much. So I offered him our home (my son and I stayed at my mother's house for the evening) and the guys grilled steaks, smoked Cuban cigars, played poker, watched a porn video or two, and then disbanded around two in the morning. I doubt the party cost more than $100, and everyone was happy.

If there's no home to have this kind of party in, renting a hotel room for the night is the next best thing. There's no cleaning up, but you do have to bring a number of things to the hotel room, such as the booze and plates (unless you want to order everything from room service, and that's just about as expensive as going to a restaurant) and then cart them all home again. You can avoid ordering food from room service by ordering pizza or Chinese takeout.

Guys don't give gifts at bachelor parties, but they may bring a bottle. Women tend to bring intimate items for the bride, like racy lingerie or funny sex-related items (chocolate body parts come to mind). Although I didn't have a cake at my bachelorette party (which consisted of a night of visiting my favorite bars in Greenwich Village), I have been to a few bachelorette parties where cake was served (this is the home-party version) and the cake itself is often a novelty item (those body parts again). One simple recipe for this kind of cake is to make a round vanilla or chocolate cake, stand a Twinkie or Devil Dog in the center, and then cover with peach or chocolate icing.

Home and hotel parties for the bachelor often feature a visit from a stripper, which is always more expensive than expected. The guys usually chip in for this among themselves, but the stripper expects a hefty tip and often charges a travel fee as well.

My husband got hoodwinked into attending a bachelor party that involved a night of going to strip clubs in New York City. The party started in a guy's house, but headed downtown around midnight, and few of the guys knew they were going to be doing this, so few of them had a lot of cash. This turned out to be a very expensive evening for everyone who attended, especially because someone had to keep tipping the strippers for paying extra attention to the groom-to-be.

Anniversary Celebrations

An anniversary party should be as extravagant as you can afford, yet still not be outrageously expensive. I was twenty-four years old when I threw my parents their twenty-fifth wedding anniversary party, and pretty close to dirt poor. Yet, through the network of family and my parent's good friends, we managed to put together a party that was as elegant as they could have hoped.

I knew I could never afford the lavish restaurant anniversary parties that some of my parents' friends' kids were throwing. One couple had theirs at Tavern on the Green in Central Park, and asked their friends to kick in a per-couple fee that included the meal and the gift. But that approach has never been right for me, and Miss Manners says that if you do the inviting, you should do the paying. I decided that making it a surprise party would be the extra ingredient. So I "borrowed" my mother's address book one afternoon and invited all of my parents' friends, both old and new, including my mom's maid of honor and my dad's best man, whom he hadn't seen for years. The party took place at my aunt's house (she had offered). The coup de grâce was that I flew my younger brother in from California for the weekend.

The menu consisted of all my parents' favorite things to eat and drink. We made some dishes ourselves and had other items catered.

My aunt knew that my mother had recently developed a passion for Lladró figurines, so she collected a small fee from the guests (she was the one they called for directions) and bought a Lladró sculpture of a bride and groom as the big anniversary present for my parents. Most anniversary parties feature some big present from the guests. It can be anything from a lovely piece of crystal to a cruise.

My aunt arranged to have music from the late fifties playing (my parents were married in 1958) and knew just the right songs to play. The guests all danced and reminisced, and it was a wonderful party on a budget.

A nice touch for an anniversary party is to order a sheet cake and have the baker use a color Xerox of the couple's wedding picture as the decoration on the cake. You can also order a three-tiered cake and use the wedding centerpiece from their original wedding cake or buy them a new one.

Another idea for the joint present is to ask each guest to bring an old photo of themselves with the anniversary couple and to write something about them. One woman painstakingly put this kind of material together on her computer and ended up making a cherished memento book for the anniversary couple and the fifty guests who attended the party.

Another unique and inexpensive idea for mementos is to have a wedding photo of the couple reproduced at the local print shop and laminated, so that you have a placemat that can be used at the anniversary party and then taken home when the guests leave. You could also make T-shirts or coffee mugs.

One anniversary party featured a slide show of the couple's wedding photos, with a commentary by the bridal party. This is a good way to bring back the memories without having to pass the wedding album around.

I recently attended a tenth anniversary party for a couple who had eloped. This time around they wanted to throw themselves as big a party as they could, so they had an outdoor party under tents in their very large backyard (there were at least one hundred people there). The food was catered, and a hired band supplied the entertainment. It was like a wedding reception, but much more laid back.

Another way to have a large anniversary party is to go back to the hall where the couple first had their reception. If you can, you might even try to reproduce the original menu and music.

Bon Voyage Party

An anniversary sometimes turns into a bon voyage party because the group gift is often a trip—a special trip that the couple has always wanted to go on. I know of one couple who had five kids and had never managed to go to Greece, where their parents were from. Their kids got together and sent them to Greece for their thirtieth anniversary as their present.

One way of making two tickets to a foreign country affordable is to get family and/or friends to "donate" airline mileage points to one sibling and then have them cash them in for two tickets. This is a lot of work, and will probably take a solid half day on the phone, but two round-trip tickets to Europe usually runs about $1,500, so it's definitely worth it if you don't have cash.

You cannot wait until the last minute to do this. It will take about six to eight weeks for the vouchers to arrive and then the person with the mileage points will have to go to a satellite airline ticket office, or an airport, to buy the tickets.

At a bon voyage party, the decorations should be themed. If you plan to buy decorations and place settings, call around to your local party stores for prices, because these are the kinds of items that are often on closeout at one store and at full price at another. Who's going to know that your decorations are last year's model?

If you want to make your own decorations, it can be something as simple as blue tablecloths to represent water with cardboard fishes glued to them and a cake in the shape of a boat if the party recipient is going on a cruise or a light blue tablecloth with white clouds and little toy airplanes on the cake.

For the more complicated version of the bon voyage party you could do something as inspired as an amateur luau for a trip to Hawaii or a menu from the country where the recipient is going (go to the library or the Internet for recipes) and artistic renderings of the country's great architectural wonders taped to the wall (such as the Eiffel Tower or the Pyramids). If you are one of those truly inspired party-throwers (who has already done this a few times for children) you could make a piñata in the shape of the architectural wonder and fill it with candy from that country (the Leaning Tower of Pisa with Perugina chocolates). You could also try to do the same with a cake. Don't forget to play music from the country to be visited (which you should be able to get from the library or a friend if you don't have some on hand).

Sometimes people bring presents to these parties, sometimes they don't. Sometimes a collection is taken to buy the party recipient a new set of luggage. Another appropriate gift is a collection of travel-related items, such as travel-size toiletries, books to read on the plane, makeup and jewelry travel cases. You might also give a little something from the place being visited, such as candy, to whet the visitor's appetite.

Graduation and Retirement Parties

Graduation and retirement parties appear to be opposite ends of the life spectrum, but are actually very similar—graduation parties represent retirement from a certain phase of schooling. They are also attended by people who have been through the trenches together—other graduating students and others in the workplace.

Because students in a class all graduate on the same day, you have to make sure that a favorite classmate's graduation party isn't scheduled for the same day as yours. By coordinating parties, you might even be able to get a few students together to share the bill. However, many graduation parties include the families who helped foot the graduate's bill through school, so be careful not to mix the wilder "I'm finally done with law school" bash with the more staid family affair.

Graduation usually entails two parties—the bash and the family celebration. The bash is usually thrown by a few students chipping in and features the ubiquitous kegs of beer, jugs of wine, chips and dip, and possibly pizza ordered in. Keep it simple and keep it plastic, because the partying is the focus, not the food or the decor.

The family celebration is a much more formal gathering—aunts and uncles who haven't been heard from since the bar mitzvah, second and third cousins twice removed—are all descending upon the graduate with presents of Parker Pen sets and envelopes of cash. Invitations to graduation parties usually come in the mail, although a homemade invitation would still be acceptable here (perhaps made to resemble a diploma).

If it's an at-home celebration, the party should take place on a Saturday afternoon, so relatives from not too far away can drive in for the day. It will probably be semicatered, featuring the big sandwich, hot plates of ziti and lasagna and meatballs, salad, bread, and a sheet cake with the word "Congratulations!" spelled out in icing. If the party takes place in June (which is when most schools let out), it could be in the backyard and might be a barbecue. Beer and soda can be set out in coolers.

If there's any decoration, it tends to be white and blue (don't ask me why), although some creative parents or friends might try to coordinate the decor with the school's colors. I have been to one party where the words "Congratulations, Graduate!" were printed out on computer paper and strung across the room as a banner—a cute way of reminding students how much time they spent at the computer. At another party, all the fancy paper napkins were rolled up as though they were diplomas.

For a centerpiece, you could buy one of the many character graduate figures (such as the Barbie graduate doll or Mickey and Minnie or even Precious Moments). If the graduate collects these kinds of mementos, you should buy a graduate figure (Lladró, Hummel, etc.) and give it to her at the end of the celebration.

You can also make a centerpiece that is relevant to the profession the graduate plans to enter—for a doctor a basket stuffed with inflated surgical gloves, bandages, a thermometer, etc., that you can put together from almost any medical cabinet or a simple visit to the local pharmacy. Same goes for an architect (slide rule, rulers, pencils, large erasers) or a lawyer (a copy of the *Law Review*, yellow legal pads, stenographer's tape). It's easy to put something together to reflect almost any profession.

The one thing I would caution against giving is the pen set or calculator. The graduate will get tens of these. I dislike giving money, but this is an occasion where I often do. It is also a good occasion to give a gift certificate or treasury bond.

When someone retires, they often get two parties—one at work and another one with family, friends, and coworkers.

The work party can be as formal as a sit-down dinner for one hundred to toast the life work of the retiree, who is then given an engraved gold watch or crystal bowl. Or it can be a dinner at a favorite restaurant near the job after the last day of work, where the coworkers get together and chip in for a last meal together. They usually buy something a little more fun like luggage (for that trip the retiree is planning) or art supplies for that hobby that he will supposedly now have more time for. Then there's lots of hugging, lots of kissing, some crying, and a lot of photos.

When my father retired from consistory after twenty-five years of service at the local church, the other consistory members threw him a dinner party for fifty. A champagne punch was served on the church lawn as the guests arrived. A bulletin was printed with the three-course menu, which also served as a memento of the occasion.

The meal was extravagant in its presentation (melon and pro-sciutto, sliced London broil with mushrooms, string beans and carrots, and individual lemon and berry tarts) because one of the newer consistory members was an amateur chef. After a performance of piano music and a recital of Broadway songs (another consistory member was a professional singer), speeches were made and my father was presented with a sculpture of the tree of life for his contributions to the church. It was a warm and touching party, and truly elegant.

However, it is usually the party with family and friends, typically thrown by the spouse or the adult kids, that really marks the entry into retirement. It usually includes a number of work-related friends or associates from over the years. It can be in a restaurant or at home and usually takes place in the afternoon or evening, featuring either a full lunch or dinner. Cocktails or punch are served. Numerous toasts are made.

I know some adult siblings who hosted a retirement party for their mother, who was a nurse. They were able to use a community room at the hospital where she worked. They made a centerpiece out of hospital supplies and asked each of their mother's friends to bring something, such as a salad or dessert. It was an extremely successful celebration.

If you are invited to a retirement party, always check to see if there is a collection for a big gift for the retiree before you go out and buy something on your own. Generally, a gift that relates to the retiree's hobby is very appropriate. It could be something as simple as two tickets to a local movie theater (most theater chains sell gift certificates) or some books that you know the person would enjoy. It could even be an IOU for a lunch in the near future, when the changing pace of the retiree's life begins to settle in.

When I was younger, I took many of these "Hallmark" occasions, and the parties that marked them, for granted. Now that I have been through a handful of these life experiences myself, and find myself either hosting these special occasion celebrations, or at least participating in them, I realize how important they are. These are the times we remember, so make the details count.

6

Parties for Family and Friends

Most of us have annual get-togethers and family obligations that we are responsible for. In my family, I'm the one who hosts the holiday dinners—Thanksgiving, Christmas, and Easter—because my mother is a minister and always has to work on those days. I have a close friend who has a wonderful trim-the-tree party every December and a cousin through marriage who invites us for a spectacular Fourth of July party every year.

Before I took over my family traditions, I remember visiting my father's sister's house in Connecticut for the holidays, but we always celebrated Greek Easter (which falls a week or two after the Roman Easter) with my mother's sister in Riverdale. When I think of each side of my family, it is those annual holiday gatherings that are the basis for most of my memories.

The same now goes for the family I married into—my mother-in-law loves to host New Year's Eve, and it "belongs" to her. When my son is grown, the family gatherings I've hosted will be the source of most of his family memories.

Since I know that every year I will be serving Thanksgiving, Christmas, and Easter dinner, I have linen and dishes and decorations galore (bought on sale the day after the holiday) for each holiday. I actually remember debating whether or not I should buy myself a porcelain Easter salt and pepper shaker set that featured a pink and blue egg nestled in a white basket. It was on sale for half price for $8 ten years ago and it was a one-day-only sale. It seemed awfully pricey for something I was only going to use once a year, but I decided to treat myself, and it has become one of my favorite Easter tablepieces (and I've certainly recouped my $8 out of it already).

My rule for seasonal entertaining is that if you are the person who hosts the annual get-togethers, the cost of special decorations will be displaced over the years. You should feel good about investing in appropriate decorations that may become family heirlooms as the years go by.

The basics for any given holiday are a tablecloth and a center-piece. Discretion is then advised regarding how many accents you want to add, such as the above-mentioned salt and pepper shakers, decorative platters, cookie jars, and mugs. One way to ensure that your holiday decor will always be plentiful is to let people know that you love adding to the existing table. You will then most likely receive decorative housewares as presents when guests visit for the holidays. However, you can only use a finite number of platters for any holiday.

Even though I host these holidays every year, I do try to have one really spectacular element each year that will set each holiday apart from the previous one. One year I made scores of Christmas cookies, which I decorated, shellacked, and gave out as presents. Another year I let the kids string tree garlands of popcorn and cranberries. I made my own gingerbread house at Christmas (or at least I tried, which was fun in itself). One Easter I hid eggs with fancy candy inside for adults.

Christmas

This is a big holiday time of the year for me, and since I have a large extended family, as does my husband, we tend to celebrate the holiday, having big and little get-togethers, throughout the season. As a result, I begin to decorate my house the first week of December (whether or not I have the tree up).

I have two Christmas tablecloths. One is a hand-me-down from my grandmother that always reminds me of holidays at her house, but it is also the less spectacular of the two, and the one I put on when young children are coming. The other is a rather expensive green tablecloth with gold and red Christmas tree embroidery that I received as a present and have used every year since it was given to me. Since we have so many gatherings, one of these two tablecloths adorns the dining room table throughout the season, and both are washed frequently. If you entertain a lot during this season I would recommend that you buy two Christmas tablecloths and alternate them. I would also recommend that you case the department stores (and favorite discount stores) and price the tablecloths before the holiday. Pick out the one you want, and then go shopping the morning after the holiday. It is almost certain to be there at half price on the twenty-sixth.

The other thing you can do is buy green and red tablecloths (or fabric) and napkins and alternate them (green tablecloth with red napkins). If you're at all artistic and want to embroider a simple Christmas tree or wreath in the corners and along the border in gold, this can really dress up your tablecloth.

Another alternative is to buy winter-themed tablecloths (snow-covered village scenes, snowmen with snow falling), which you can use for the holidays and throughout the winter months. Yards of dark fabric, in navy blue or deep purple, can also be used, perhaps with a lace runner.

I have a full collection of Christmas tableware that I have amassed over the years. Some have been gifts; others I have bought for myself. I use them all. In my family, I am considered one of the Christmas queens.

My Christmas collection consists of a set of dishes, which were a present, a set of glasses and mugs (also presents), a Santa cookie jar, and a special plate where we place the cookies for Santa on Christmas Eve (bought on December 26 for $3), three platters, candlesticks, a teapot, and a ceramic bread basket. The bread basket and candlesticks or the cookie jar are usually my centerpieces. I consider this to be a fairly full table and rarely put all this Christmas fare out at the same time.

However, I list these items as suggestions for family presents as well, because you can usually pick them up at after-Christmas sales and save them for the next year. Occasionally you may be able to find a Lenox Christmas piece for sale at a yard sale or flea market. Buy it and give it to someone who loves Christmas. They won't care if it's used, because these items go for up to $100 each in department stores.

I don't like to clutter my house with too many Christmas knick-knacks. Aside from my Christmas tree, I put a reusable wreath on my door, a Christmas towel in my guest bathroom, and I hang the Christmas cards I've received around the fireplace mantel.

Although my Christmas wreath is store-bought, my mother used to make beautiful Christmas wreaths to sell at my annual school fair, and everyone bought them. She would buy styrofoam bases from an arts and craft or floral supply store and then glue on acorns, pine cones, "itchy balls," and walnuts and spray paint the whole thing gold. She would finish the wreath with a glued-on red velvet bow. You can also make candlestick wreaths this way.

The towel I put in my guest bathroom at Christmastime is also handmade. Someone took a red towel and stitched a cutout of a green Christmas tree to the terry cloth. It adds a nice touch to the holiday season.

I host a number of get-togethers and parties over the Christmas season from breakfast to dessert, and attend a few gatherings as well.

One of my best friends hosts an annual trim-the-tree dinner around the third week of December. Guests bring ornaments for her tree and we decorate the tree while we eat. She always makes a homemade eggnog and the food is usually a spread of pasta, salads, vegetables, and various hors d'oeuvres. Everything is served on red and green plastic plates.

I usually have a buffet for my husband's cousins and their kids before Christmas, at which we exchange gifts. Because the holiday season is so hectic (often this party is on a Friday night), and we all have so many events to attend this time of the year, I might ask some of my guests to bring dessert or a side dish. I'll usually serve some sort of casserole, salad, and garlic bread, and then a big dessert spread with a pie and homemade cookies. I might buy the seasonal ice cream cake (using a coupon) that is featured at the local Carvel or Baskin-Robbin's for the kids.

I love cooking the Christmas dinner, but I'm also usually exhausted from the shopping and wrapping of the days before. Therefore, I always make the same meal, because I can do it with my eyes closed: turkey, Greek salad, stuffed celery, mashed potatoes and stuffing, with the leftover desserts from the other parties during Christmas week. I might add some store-bought baklava ($7 at the local Greek store or $6 at Costco, which feeds twelve). I stock plenty of sparkling apple cider at this time of year.

For entertaining at home, my husband and I have collected an assortment of Christmas music, which spans the standards of Handel's *Messiah* and Perry Como/Bing Crosby classics to Christmas rock and rap. We place three Christmas CDs on the stereo and let them play as background music throughout these gatherings.

Some people don't like to have the same Christmas party year after year. Thankfully, there are many variations on the Christmas theme. I've read of Christmas fiestas, where the food featured is Mexican (do-it-yourself fajitas and quesadillas) with a holiday piñata for the kids. In the Caribbean, people don't celebrate Christmas, but the arrival of the Three Kings. The meal is traditionally a roasted pig (*pernil*) with meat pies, rice, and plantains. There are even special candies reserved especially for this time of year, such as Spanish nougat (*turron*).

Other Christmas party variations include Christmas luaus (lots of pineapple and coconut drinks and menu items), a Tex-Mex Christmas (barbecued ribs and refried beans), or a Victorian Christmas party (plum pudding, lace doilies around a Christmas tea).

You could also serve traditional Christmas foods from around the world. Try everything from French log cake to English Christmas puddings.

Women's magazines put out annual issues fat with Christmas recipes and decorating ideas. An afternoon in the local library is certain to give you ideas, as will a ride through cyberspace looking for "Christmas recipes."

Thanksgiving

For me, Thanksgiving is a lot like Christmas, except I have the whole day to prepare.

I have been making the Thanksgiving dinner since I was twenty-two years old (which was quite a few years ago), but it wasn't until I had a child that I broke down and bought myself a Thanksgiving tablecloth. I am so glad I did. I can't tell you the number of white linen tablecloths that were ruined by gravy and/or wine stains because I was unable to accept I would probably be doing this holiday for the rest of my life. Being frugal, I didn't want to just buy a tablecloth for the one day, so I waited until I found the perfect fall tablecloth, which is green, mustard, and orange with leaves and threads of gold. Very classy, as well as being practical and cheap (only $6.99). Also, it is easy to clean and hard to stain. I also bought some Pilgrim candles and candlesticks at the local dollar store.

Fall is a wonderful time of year for fruit and vegetables that make great food as well as interesting art. Martha Stewart's simple carved apple candleholders are perfect for the Thanksgiving centerpiece. Just hollow out most of a polished apple's core (and sprinkle with lemon juice afterward, so the apple doesn't turn brown) and use it as a candlestick.

You can also dress up the table with an artistically laid out array of fall vegetables, such as small gourds and pumpkins, corn on the cob, and apples. A linen-lined basket of homemade bread also makes a nice centerpiece for this holiday.

I have a large white platter with a turkey embossed on it that I always use on Thanksgiving. I have also kept my son's Thanksgiving art from earlier years and always put something he made out for display—the turkey handprint or a feathered turkey.

My Thanksgiving meal is as traditional as it gets, and rarely varies. I make a turkey, cornbread stuffing, cranberry sauce, mashed potatoes and baked sweet potatoes, Greek salad, stuffed celery, and a pumpkin pie with whipped cream for dessert. The Grand Union where I shop offers a free turkey with a $75 purchase, a deal no cheapskate can turn down.

As with Christmas, it's not hard to vary the traditional for something different for this holiday. You could try to make your meal even more authentic, finding Colonial recipes (I believe the first Thanksgiving had a lot more fish than we realize) or interesting recipe variations for the traditional ingredients of turkey, cranberries, pumpkin, and cornmeal. You can even replace the turkey with other fowl such as goose, duck, Cornish hens, quail, or even pheasant, or try a vegetarian Thanksgiving. The Internet is a great place to go for this kind of information. In 1998 epicurious.com featured sixteen different Thanksgiving recipes from Colonial Boston to Shaker.

Easter

When I think of Easter, I think of spring flowers, egg hunts, and sumptuous Easter baskets. I believe these elements should be part of this holiday whether or not it has any religious significance for you and regardless of whether there are children around.

Since my mother is a minister, I always spend Easter morning in church. The church I attend has a policy whereby you buy an Easter lily to decorate the altar on Easter Sunday ($14 each) and then take it home after the service. I think this is a nice way to make a donation to my church and have a beautiful plant in my home for the rest of spring.

My Easter table is decorated by a pastel tablecloth of pink, lavender, blue, and white squares with matching napkins. I use these linens all spring. I have two ceramic Easter baskets made by a family friend in which I place Easter eggs and fresh bread, and salt and pepper shakers. It's a fairly simple table, but always looks lovely and very springlike.

Spring is a time of pastel colors and the table cover can be any combination of shades of lavender, pale yellow, peach, etc. Flowers make a beautiful centerpiece this time of year, from the more traditional Easter lilies and lilacs, to simple daisies and even wildflowers. Baskets lined with pastel fabric (or a linen napkin) and brimming with dyed eggs, fresh baked bread, or fruit (especially strawberries) make wonderful table accents.

My Easter dinner is pretty standard much the same every year but I believe everyone looks forward to it. I roast a leg of lamb in garlic and oregano and serve it with oven-browned potatoes, the famous Greek salad, Greek cheeses and olives, cheese pies, and grape leaves stuffed with rice (store-bought).

A baked ham, another traditional Easter entrée, can sometimes be obtained free with a purchase of $75 or more at a local supermarket. Dessert can be fruit pies, or you might want to try something a little ethnic, such as baklava or Italian pastries. Sugar cookies in the shape of bunnies always go over well, even with adults. You can buy cookie cutters at a discount store or make your own designs out of cardboard, though these can't be used year after year.

Many families have a tradition of dying eggs for this holiday. My son and I spend an evening during Easter week applying store-bought colored dyes and commercial stickers to two dozen eggs that I've hard-boiled. It really doesn't matter what size these eggs are because they are mostly for display. I buy my dyes and stickers at the dollar store and save what I don't use for the next year. However, you can make the same Easter egg dyes as those sold commercially by adding a few drops of vinegar and food coloring to a glass of water.

One of the centerpieces of my Easter table is a basket filled with the Easter eggs we have dyed. Before the night is over, we put some of the hard-boiled eggs in the salad. We have a Greek tradition of egg smashing that is supposed to bring good luck to the one whose egg holds up the best. So we smash each other's eggs (one at a time, first one side, then the next) and the one with the least damaged egg will have the best luck. We then put the eggs in the salad.

Since I usually have at least two dozen Easter eggs, I serve deviled eggs as an appetizer on this holiday. You can dress up deviled eggs by adding caviar or smoked bacon bits on top of the filing. We also have a lot of egg salad for lunch in the days following the holiday, and I often give out eggs to guests as they're leaving.

We have an Easter egg hunt for my son in the morning when he wakes up (before church). One year I bought two dozen plastic Easter eggs (dollar store again: I got two dozen for a dollar), and I now reuse them every year. You can put almost anything you want inside: chocolate-covered eggs, gold coins, miniature peanut butter cups, or jelly beans. Easter egg hunts for adults can feature pieces of paper with prizes, fortunes placed in the eggs, or expensive chocolates, such as Perugina.

There is no reason to resort to a store-bought Easter basket, unless you don't have the time to put one together. You can pick up a basket at any dollar store, and Easter grass is usually 50 cents a bag.

My son loves it when I fill his basket with small items from the dollar store: Superman comics, a Spalding ball, a paddle and ball, Silly Putty, bubbles. You might want to make your own cookies and put a few in. I wrap the whole basket with tinted cellophane and tie it with a ribbon (one roll will last years, and you can find coupons for these). I reuse his basket every year, as well.

My mother tells of how my artistically inclined grandmother used to make Easter baskets out of cookie dough and fill them with dyed eggs, Easter chocolate, an orange, and one special toy, such as a small doll.

My son gets an Easter basket every year from neighbors and his grandmothers, so I've taken the baskets and used them throughout the house. We use one for ripening fruit in our kitchen; another for notepads, pens, tape, and scissors near the kitchen phone; and one in each bathroom to hold brushes, combs, and other grooming supplies. I also save them to put together my own gift baskets, sometimes as presents for my mother on Valentine's Day or Mother's Day.

Adult Birthday Parties

Adult birthday parties are usually thrown to mark a special birthday, such as a fortieth or sixty-fifth. I don't remember going to a lot of birthday parties before my friends and I started hitting thirty. I think this was because we were self-conscious about throwing our own parties and had not yet hooked up with someone we could get to do it for us, and we were all pretty broke.

Thirtieth and fortieth birthday parties are especially fun. They should be a little wacky and truly memorable. One of the ways to do this is to try to make the party a surprise, although the recipient often has an inkling that it's coming. If you do manage to make it a true surprise, you get extra points.

I was the first in my crowd to turn thirty, so my husband threw me a "surprise" party (although I was suspicious because he got two of my good friends to take me out to dinner on a Saturday night to keep me occupied while he put it all together). My husband managed to round up a number of friends I had not seen since college, which was a real joy, and one of my high school friends brought old pictures, which were a thrill to look at.

The menu was pretty easy, because people would be coming and going over a long period of time. My husband made his famous four-alarm chili, salad, and bread, and margaritas for one and all (my favorite drink). He ordered an ice cream cake, which I like, because it feeds so many.

Two years later, it was his turn, and I really wanted to make his thirtieth party a surprise, so I had it in my office (I own my own business), which was in an apartment, so I had a kitchen. I made tons of *chicarones de pollo* (Dominican fried chicken), which is delicious hot or cold, rice and beans, and salad. I filled the bathtub with beer on ice and bought huge jugs of white and red wine, and had a sheet cake. I got in touch with friends my husband hadn't seen in years and invited most of the people he worked with (all by phone). The party would have been a complete surprise if the doorman hadn't asked my husband if he was going to the party on his way in.

One of the things that turned out to be quite funny was the opening of the presents. I had invited a number of my husband's cousins and they brought him gag gifts like Polident, Depends, and Grecian Formula 409. I always do this now when I'm invited to a thirtieth birthday party (by the fortieth, it's not so funny).

I also threw my husband a surprise birthday party when he turned thirty-five, because I knew he wasn't expecting it. I threw it on the weekday his birthday fell on, and invited only a few close friends, but I flew his mother in from Miami. It was quite a surprise.

My mother threw my father a surprise party when he turned forty. I remember her hiding bottles of booze behind the curtains and conspiring with friends to get him out of the house while she prepared everything. He kept on asking her why she had so much food that he liked, and she kept on making up inane answers, but he believed them and was surprised.

Getting the birthday boy or girl out of the house is often one of the most difficult parts of throwing a surprise party. So something like tickets to a ballgame (as a birthday present) are a nice way to circumvent this, as are conspiracies with friends and relatives (a shopping spree, mother/daughter lunch).

For my best friend's husband's fortieth birthday, she planned a surprise "this-is-your-life" party, complete with written memories from friends that were bound into a book. She had coordinated this by mail months in advance.

Other friends have marked the coming of their fortieth birthday with an all-day, adults-only excursion, such as a weekend in Atlantic city or Las Vegas, a day at a spa, a golf marathon, hiking, or even deep sea-fishing. Less expensive ways to do something like this are to find out the group rates for things like a day at the local amusement park (Six Flags or even something like Disney World) or a Broadway play or even the big summer movie. It's fun to experience these kinds of things in an adult group (the last time you did something like this was probably high school), and you won't easily forget what you did on that birthday.

I read about one woman who threw a coworker a fiftieth birthday party at McDonald's and told the establishment it was for a kid, so they gave them all goodie bags and balloons. A hilarious time was said to have been had by all.

You can also have a kids-themed party for an adult at home, with party hats, goodie bags, and childish games like pin the tail on the donkey and musical chairs for adults. Maybe even spin the bottle (it depends on your crowd). Don't forget to make ice cream sodas!

By the time my dad reached sixty, we wanted to throw him an elegant birthday party. He loved to dance, so we found a Hilton Hotel nearby that had a live band on Friday and Saturday nights and booked a table for thirty. We invited his very best friends (many of whom had already retired and moved to Florida) and had a black-tie party that was quite fancy, like a small wedding. My uncle (retired to Florida) sent him a singing birthday telegram, which he adored (we had to clear it with the Hilton first because they were afraid she would be a stripper). My mom, brother, and I split the cost, which was about $60 a couple.

For my mom's sixty-fifth birthday this year, we had a party for one hundred in the community room of one of her churches. It was an afternoon buffet with a sheet cake and champagne punch. Presents for this party were often senior citizen–related, but fun, such as a book about deals you can't get unless you're over fifty, her New York City half-fare card (I did the paperwork for her), a subscription to

Modern Maturity, membership to AARP, and lots of discount tickets she could only get once she was sixty-five.

One woman I read about had a sixtieth birthday party with a six-ties theme (1960s, that is). You can certainly do the same for any decade.

Family Reunions

While whole books have been written about planning family reunions, I think it is possible to sum up the strategy for making these big family gatherings successful—plan every detail and make sure you have enough activities to do. Then have a back-up plan in case it rains.

Family reunions are typically attended by between fifty and one hundred people. While they are occasionally held at the ancestral home (if there's enough land), they are more likely to be held in a national park in the summer (often the Fourth of July weekend, when everyone will have a long weekend), where family members can camp out and all the descendants can run free and keep busy. National parks are cheap (a $10 entry fee for the week, and separate, usually moderate, camping fees) and they come fully stocked with picnic tables, bathrooms, and barbecue grills (not to mention lakes for swimming, fishing, and canoeing).

Sometimes, a family resort is chosen as the central location (a dude ranch, a hotel in the mountains), where the staff will help you put the reunion together and you can get a group rate. If you go off-season (September or early June) rates are lower. A family reunion should be planned at least six months ahead of time by written invi-tation (although it can be a simple photocopied one). A lot of the follow-up can be done by E-mail.

One woman asked each branch of the family to send photos and write a brief history, which she put together as a memento. Another family reunion featured a lecture and slide show on the family history from collected stories and photos. Another family put all the history together and made their own family version of Trivial Pursuit. Some families have asked everyone for their best or favorite recipes and put together a family cookbook. One family asked each branch to sew a square for a giant family quilt to be stitched together at the reunion.

Another reunion featured different color T-shirts for each branch of the family (there were five grandparents, each represented by a different color with the first name of the grandparent on the back, so that everyone wearing a purple T-shirt featuring the letter C belonged to Clara's clan.)

Food for these large crowds can be an enormous amount of work. If you hold the reunion in a park, you can either make each family responsible for their own food or assign different families to cook different meals at different times. Everything can be barbecued or cooked on the grill.

A family reunion is a great place to play all those outdoor games you see in old movies—potato-sack races, egg rolls, horseshoe pitching, even croquet. Then there's also volleyball, softball, badminton, and Frisbee. Of course, the entire reunion should be documented in photos and video. You could also put together scrapbooks for those who attended or make copies of the videotape.

It's a lot of work to bring many people from different states together every year, and sometimes it's not appreciated if the family members do this too often. One family reunion I know about is held every five years, so that members will make an effort to attend and they can really see the changes in the family over each five-year span.

Holidays, birthdays, and family gatherings are the most common reasons why we all get together, but these events should never be taken for granted. Imagination and good planning can make up for a small budget, and you can give parties that people will remember fondly for years.

7

Odd Occasion Parties

These are the parties that your friends and family will remember until their dying days, and the stories they tell about these events may even become part of the family lore (hopefully it won't be about someone's behavior at one of these parties, but that's another book). These are also the parties that take the most work, because there is so much creativity involved. They should also be the parties that you enjoy the most.

Sometimes these are parties with a purpose, such as raising money for the rent or moving, and sometimes they're just for the the fun of it, like a treasure hunt or a masquerade ball or a luau. If you love a certain time of year (Halloween or the Fourth of July) or type of dress ('20s, Victorian), these parties can be opportunities to let that fantasy come alive. Some people even tie these parties into a special birthday theme (your husband's fortieth birthday set on the starship *Enterprise*).

Sweet 16

I'm not sure teenage girls even celebrate this birthday in a big way anymore, but when I remember back to my Sweet 16 party, it was my parents who wanted it, not me. It was more a milestone that *they* were celebrating than one that I was celebrating for myself.

My parents invited twelve of my best friends to our home for a buffet dinner of turkey and a homemade cake with peppermint icing that my mother still won't let me forget. Then we all went to see the Broadway play *Grease.* My Dad bought me a wrist corsage with six-teen pieces of Bazooka bubble gum on it. You can easily make this or a variation on it with your daughter's favorite candy wired to fresh or silk flowers on a wrist band.

By the time your daughter hits her teen years, the last thing she will want to do is spend her birthday with the family. But Sweet 16 can be a memorable marker, and for many (including myself) it may turn out to be the only large birthday party for her friends during the high school years. The pictures alone will be worth it years from now.

A variation on this theme is the slumber party, usually for a small group (four to six). One of my best friends from high school had about six of us sleep over for her Sweet 16, which was quite memorable, because by sixteen we had all stopped having slumber parties. Her parents took us to an art gallery opening (very grown-up for us) and then we went back to their house for more grown-up partying and dinner. I remember being very impressed that they had put out an entire spread of appetizers just for us (it was the first time I had Genoa salami and cream cheese roll-ups, which I love). Her dad took a terrific black-and-white group photo of us with our long hair and jeans, mounted it on cardboard, and gave it to us a few weeks later. It was a wonderful memento and I still have it on my dresser after all these years.

Sweet 16 parties can be a wonderful occasion to mark the transition from teen to adult in a very feminine way. Now that I'm older, I truly value this marker, and would recommend that parents try to make a special occasion for their daughters, even if it's only a family party with her favorite meal.

Throwing an adult party for your teenager is one way to make her feel that she is indeed growing up. You could serve a very fancy dinner for her friends (something French or Italian) with the (nonalcoholic) drinks in wine goblets or champagne glasses. Put out the fine linen, china, and silver, and offer a truly elegant dessert of chocolate mousse or a soufflé.

An alternative to this approach is to let your daughter put together the menu and have the teens all cook it themselves (with your supervision). It can be something as simple as fajitas or as complicated as chicken tarragon. You could also try cooking a new type of cuisine, such as Chinese, Thai, or Japanese, which could be fun. The photos from this party will be prized possessions, so make multiple copies for her friends.

Other Sweet 16 party ideas include a makeover party, where friends go to a department store and have their makeup done by a professional. Perhaps you also buy each teen a small cosmetic, which should entitle them to the free gift that comes with the purchase. You could also hire a beauty school student to come to the house for a consultation. Facials, manicures, and pedicures are fun group activities.

Craft Parties

While most of us have been to arts and craft parties for kids, which are always fun because we get to watch children making Christmas ornaments, T-shirts, and ceramics, a well-planned adult craft party is always memorable for both the guests and the hostess.

A traditional type of craft gathering is a quilting party. The hostess must decide on what type of quilt will be made and the pattern. There are so many varieties on quilt-making today that the hostess must make this decision before the party. If you need help on deciding, or putting the materials together, there are ample resources on the Internet, as well as many quilting books in the library. An easy idea for a quilt party is denim quilts, using pieces of different worn-out jeans and flannel sheets as the backing.

Most quilting parties require that each guest bring a certain amount of fabric, and then they cut and stitch and trade until the quilts are complete. This takes an afternoon or slightly longer, and a full lunch should be served, which might include salad sandwiches. If the party has been called to make a quilt for a purpose (such as a bridal or baby shower gift made by friends or family), you might serve a cake with an appropriate motif.

Once known as quilting bees, these parties are the kinds of events that women's groups in the local church used to do in an afternoon before the church fair, and many churches still have craft-making afternoons. However, you can do the same thing before a bridal or baby shower and present the bride or mother-to-be with a trove of handmade gifts that are priceless. These include embroidered tablecloths and matching napkins, crocheted or knit baby clothes, and homemade housewares such as pot holders and tissue covers. You can get inspiration from back issues of women's magazines, craft magazines, and books from the library, as well as Internet sources.

Another craft party could involve making Christmas decorations, either to be sold at a local fund-raising event or for each participant to take home. The hostess must provide all the basic art supplies and ask each guest to bring something special for the craft, such as feathers, sequins, odd buttons, beads, or glitter to add variety to the decorations. You can make ornaments, wreaths, and even complicated ceramics like a Christmas village or a nativity, which can be ordered from a craft store and then decorated at the party. You can even make and shellac cookie ornaments. Some women's groups make Christmas pies and fruit cakes and sell or raffle them at a bazaar.

When I was a teenager, my aunt belonged to a sewing circle. They would get together monthly to swap patterns and trade material or buy it as a group. They did most of the sewing at home on machines, but they finished the clothing at the circle, taking up hems and sewing in zippers and buttons. They also used the sewing circle to trade buttons and zippers and other stuff, as well as enjoying it as a social gathering.

The kind of party I used to love was getting together with four or five of my girlfriends to tie-dye pieces of clothing—anything from T-shirts to bathing suits. For baby boomers, this would make a great activity now, with our own teenage kids and their friends, or with now-adult friends from our own teenage years.

Tie-dye kits are sold at just about every craft store and you can pick up men's plain white T-shirts for a buck or two at outlets and discount stores. Go through all the white and light-colored cotton clothes and stained table linen and sheets you have that you've been meaning to throw out and dump them all in the dye. You'd be surprised how interesting things can get. Kids especially just love tie-dyed sheets.

Treasure Hunt

I went to a treasure hunt hosted by a friend of my roommate when I was in college. Clues were placed all over Roosevelt Island (an island on the East River) on the Friday night of a Halloween weekend. Even though it was cold out, and I was running around a part of New York I was unfamiliar with in a costume that had high heels and uncomfortable clothing, I had a great time. The host placed clues in the empty community pool, on the inside of a bell, and on the sign of an abandoned insane asylum. It was the kind of setting great slasher movies are based on, and perfect for a Halloween party. The first team to find all the clues got tickets to a Broadway show.

There's a really bad '80s teen movie about a treasure hunt called *Midnight Madness,* which inspired my husband and me to throw a Manhattan treasure hunt for our friends when we were in our mid-twenties. We invited about thirty people, broke them into teams of four or five, and had each person put $10 into a kitty that would be the prize for the winning team. We gave them the rules of the hunt at a cocktail-like party (lots of appetizers) and gave each team eight dimes for phone calls. We sent them out into the world at about three o'clock and told everyone to come back to our place by eight whether or not a team had won (where we would give them all dinner—our famous chili).

It took my husband and me about two weeks to come up with the clues for the party, which we placed on stickers we attached to objects in public areas. We had to come up with eight locations everyone would know and then figure out a way to place the clues so that our friends could find them. At a few places we called the management to ask for help, and if they refused, we just put the stickers (white Avery labels) in the men's and ladies' rooms.

This party was a lot of work, but the most fun we ever had. It took us about two weeks to come up with the clues and we spent the entire day before the party running around Manhattan placing clues on landmarks.

We came up with eight locations: Grant's Tomb, P.J. Clarke's, Port Authority, and Fraunces Tavern were four of them and clues (anagrams, puzzles, word games; one was Scrabble letters in an envelope). The clue for P.J. Clarke's (a famous, old New York bar) was "Superman in his pajamas, ass backwards." Each team was to call in when they got to the site to confirm. If they couldn't get the clue in an hour, we would give them the next clue and they would lose a point. The clue to the next site was located somewhere on the site they were calling from. We handed them their first clue (the Scrabble letters in an envelope).

We didn't know how long it would take for a team to figure everything out, but the first team came back around 7:00 P.M. We all had a blast.

You can also put together a scavenger hunt where you give a list of oddball items (a simple list like a horse, train, cloud, or a weird-themed list from literature or popular culture like eye of Newt, witches' brew, bell, book, and candle) and give your guests a time limit to bring everything back with rules that all items must be found, not bought. If your hunt is over a holiday, you can make the items coordinate with the holiday theme.

A little creativity in putting the list together will go a long way in making the hunt fun. A great prize as the reward makes people work that much harder and take the whole thing a little more seriously. Cash (the kitty idea), theater tickets, a gift certificate to a great local restaurant, are all good suggestions for this sort of thing.

Masquerades and Costume Parties

I love masquerades and costume parties but find that as I get older my friends don't throw them anymore. In fact, it is easy to throw a costume party, and relatively inexpensive. The guests, and their costumes, are the theme and the entertainment, although you still have to supply the food and music.

If you're planning on having twenty-five people or under, throw it in your home. For more than that, rent a small space, like the community room in a co-op. Our co-op hosted a costume party this year, serving mulled wine and cider and roast beef and turkey as the dinner. They had a best costume contest and showed *The Rocky Horror Picture Show* on the VCR (they have a big-screen TV), which was a great idea. When I was a kid, we used to dunk for apples with dimes in them (you need quarters or Susan B. Anthony dollars today), which I think would be a riot for adults to do.

You could also have a themed costume party, either tied to the holiday you're celebrating (an *Addams Family* Halloween party, Colonial Fourth of July, futuristic New Year's party) or the theme of the party (by decade, a *Titanic* party, a *Star Trek* party, where everyone comes in a Starfleet uniform).

Masquerades are fancy costume parties where everyone is expected to wear a mask and elegant attire or a costume. These are the kinds of parties where you really should send out fancy invitations, hire musicians (or at least a neighborhood kid who can play the violin or piano), and maybe even hire a few teenagers in black pants and white shirts to serve hors d'oeuvres. A spring or summer masquerade could be on the lawn or backyard of a large home (borrowed or rented). Though not the least expensive way to entertain, you can keep the cost of an elegant masquerade down by serving punches and the upscale version of the less expensive appetizers (deviled eggs with caviar). It is the illusion of elegance that is required here, not the actual credit card receipts.

Theme Parties for Adults

The great thing about theme parties is that if you place most of your energy into the theme and its execution, you won't have to spend a lot of money on impressing or entertaining your guests. A successful theme party will do that for you, so you can have a good time.

There are so many varieties for adult parties from the simple (a silly hat party) to the sublime (a Vegas night). Often a theme party is tied to a birthday, which can be a lot of fun. Just make sure your friends know that there is a theme to the party (I would recommend written invitations for this kind of party) or someone is likely to feel left out. Just in case, you can always keep extra items on hand to include anyone who forgot, such as extra silly hats.

Some simple and successful themes are a pajama party (with breakfast-related food even though the party's at night), a toga party (I understand that the guests are not supposed to wear underwear at the more traditional toga parties, which is why these were so popular on college campuses), a Mardi Gras party (jambalaya, red beans and rice, pitchers of Hurricanes), or a fiesta (tacos, nachos, do-it-yourself fajitas, pitchers of margaritas and a piñata filled with candy or adult prizes).

Decade parties are easy-to-throw theme parties. Guests come in the clothing of the decade, you play the music from the decade, and try to serve the food and drinks from that time. If you have a large-screen TV, you can show classic movies from the decade (with the sound turned down so as not to distract your guests).

A '20s speakeasy party could include guests dressed up as gangsters, gun molls, and flappers with Prohibition-style mixed drinks and bottles of gin on ice in the bathtub. A '30s party could feature dance music and a request that guests dress like Fred and Ginger. A '40s party should feature swing music and guests in uniforms from WWII. A '50s party could be a *Happy Days* set, with leather jackets and poodle skirts, burgers and malteds and early rock'n'roll. For the '60s, a menu of spiked Tang and Cheetos could accompany a soundtrack from the Beatles to the Cowsills (remember them?) with guests in bell bottoms and tie-dyes. The '70s would be a disco party (your own private Studio 54), with pitchers of Harvey Wallbangers, fondue, quiche, and onion dip, leisure suits and lycra dresses. You get the idea, I'm sure. Of course, you can go even farther back in time or even to another country (Edwardian England, Revolutionary France).

One woman had a *Casablanca* surprise birthday party for her husband. She had all the guests come in period clothing, rented roulette and poker tables, made armbands for the dealers, borrowed fezzes from a local mens' club, had someone playing the piano, and transformed her home into the nightclub from her husband's favorite movie.

Another woman turned her home into a Las Vegas nightclub, with poker and blackjack tables, and music by Elvis, Sinatra, and Cher.

It is easy to come up with a theme around someone's favorite movie or TV show, from *Star Wars* (reproduce the famous bar scene and buy plates and tablecloths that are made for children's parties) to *Star Trek* (there's even a *Star Trek* cookbook; make your guests improvise those costumes—this could be a riot) to a *Seinfeld* party (you can probably get ideas for this online, but it should be in a crowded apartment with lots of cereal boxes).You could even do a *Gone With the Wind* party with a Southern theme and serve mint juleps.

Other parties I've heard about have been a vintage prom night, where the couples are expected to come in thrift-shop prom gowns and tuxes, wearing corsages. Lots of slow-dancing songs are played. Give out tacky prom mementos at the end of the evening.One couple hosted a Valentine's Day party that was black tie and had a theme of wine and roses.

Sales Parties

These are really fund-raising parties where you sell your friends things that you hope they will need, or at least want, such as Avon, Amway, Tupperware, Discovery Toys, or lingerie. I've actually had a good time at these parties when I've known ahead of time that I was going to be pitched to. However, when I went without a warning that these were sales parties,that has really ticked me off.My rule of thumb: always let your guests know what to expect,preferably with a written invitation. They are more likely to bring money, checkbooks, and credit cards if you let them know ahead of time, which should improve your sales record.

A good sales party will have a nice spread for the guests, either appetizers or a light lunch. Because you're asking your guests to spend money, you should make sure that everything looks top quality (so no generic brands on display here).

You should try to have about ten or twelve people at the sales party, including some relatives whom you've primed to buy something from you, so that you and your guests won't be embarrassed if they don't buy anything.

Housewarming Parties

Housewarming parties can be a lot of fun for both the hosts and the guests.A housewarming party should be by invitation.A lot of people may want to come and see the new house or apartment or co-op (especially if they've been hearing the details about how you got your mortgage or your move or your renovation), but won't drop by without an invitation. However, many people refrain from throwing house-warming parties because they're afraid it will seem as though they're asking for gifts. If you really don't want gifts, you can put that on the invitation. Some people register at gift stores for their house needs (it works like a bridal registry), but you should never put this on the invitation. If you want people to get you something from your registry, have a subtle relative or friend be in charge of spreading the word.

You could also have a themed housewarming party, such as home improvement (where you'll get tools, gift certificates to Home Depot) or garden (planters, gardening tools, plants).

One couple wanted to have a casual after-dinner housewarming party where friends could drop in any time from 7:00 to 11:00 P.M. On the invitation they wrote, "Please 'warm' our new home and enjoy coffee and dessert with us." This way, the guests knew what to expect.

The food for a housewarming can be as simple as the coffee and dessert mentioned above or a big barbecue or a potluck supper (this is actually a very good excuse for a potluck). It's really up to you.

Potluck Parties

Potluck dinners and parties have the reputation of being thrown together almost at the last minute. But the best bring-your-own-food gatherings I've ever attended have always been well coordinated.

Whether for 12 or 200 (church functions and school socials), a good hostess or coordinator gets on the phone and finds out what people are bringing and makes sure that there are not too many desserts and no main dishes. If the party appears to be heavy on side dishes, she might ask you to make your famous Greek meatballs, ensuring that there's the right balance of food for the party. The hostess is also responsible for supplying drinks (which includes alcoholic and nonalcoholic beverages, as well as after-dinner coffee and tea) and table settings.

A potluck gathering for more than a dozen people should be by invitation, and then followed up by phone. The written invitation should state that you need to know what the guest is bringing when she RSVPs.

As with all dinner parties, great entertaining is in the details.

Because your guests are supplying most of the food, you can really splurge on one or two things, such as champagne with dessert or shrimp cocktail appetizers. You can also use the opportunity to prepare a really complicated dessert or appetizer because you don't have to cook the entire meal.

Potlucks are also wonderful for when you really do want to get together with friends but your schedule is too hectic to take a day to do the cooking. It's nice to share your friends' food at your table and it gives you the opportunity to try different things.

If you're harried for the holidays and you have a lot of family to invite, a potluck meal could be a new tradition. If you supply the main course (the turkey, ham, or lamb), your guests can round out the meal with fabulous side dishes.

The church I grew up in has an annual potluck supper with the theme "international night." This is a great way to bring people together and to sample a wide variety of delicious foods. This concept would also work well for an office potluck during lunch or just after work, especially around the holidays.

Potluck gatherings are a relaxed way to bring friends together, not to mention the least expensive way to entertain.

8

Outdoor Parties

For most of us, outdoor parties are summer gatherings, because that's
the only time of the year we can depend on nice weather. While there
are those who are quite capable of throwing elegant parties outdoors,
such as weddings under tents and fancy catered garden parties (or a
tenth anniversary party, as I described earlier), these are not the most
economical ways to entertain (although it does save the cost of renting a hall). Most of us use the excuse to be outdoors as an opportunity to make the entertaining more casual, so most outdoor parties I
go to, and certainly the ones I host, are barbecues, picnics, or pool
parties.

Barbecues

A barbecue can be as simple as a weenie roast over a beach bonfire
or a more complicated marinated steak on skewers affair with hired
help doing the cooking. It's really up to your needs.

One woman on a frugality newsgroup I belong to said she invited
family and friends to open-fire weenie roasts (bring your own hot
dogs and lawn chairs to sit around the fire). The host supplied the
sticks, toppings (relish, sauerkraut, ketchup, cheese sauce), and drinks,
and marshmallows for dessert.

The same couple regularly hosts potato roasts (foil provided). The wrapped potatoes are placed on open coals that are covered and uncovered by a shovel. Toppings for the potatoes, such as sour cream, cheddar cheese, bacon bits, and jalapeño peppers, are also provided by the host. These roasts are most popular in the fall, with guests sitting around the open fire, sometimes telling ghost stories.

We have barbecues almost every weekend in the summer, starting with Memorial Day, because we have a pool in the city. At the beginning of the summer I'm thrilled to be grilling hamburgers and hot dogs again and making vats of potato salad, but by the Fourth of July I'm craving variety, and we begin experimenting with easy marinades on chicken and steak and grilling tuna steaks.

I do have basic barbecue meats in the freezer at all times in the summer: ready-made hamburger patties, lots of hot dogs, and buns for both. Sirloin patties are $6.99 for eighteen at my local wholesale club. I find two-for-one specials on hot dogs at the supermarket all summer long. Hamburger and hot dog buns can be bought at a wholesale club at a price of sixteen rolls at $1.69. I find cheese doesn't freeze well, so I tend to buy it fresh.

In the summer, I buy big jars of mayonnaise (for all the potato salad and cole slaw) and bigger jars of mustard. I also buy lemons by the bagful (five pounds for $2.89, or about thirty) and boxes of one hundred tea bags (you can get a good brand for as little as a $1), and keep pitchers of homemade iced tea and lemonade. Limeade is great too and is even cheaper to make than lemonade. Every weekend I also make two to three pounds of potato salad and my husband is in charge of the cole slaw, which is easy to make from scratch and is incredibly delicious. Large cans of baked beans are available at the wholesale club (116 ounces for $3.99, which should last the summer), if this is something you like. When corn is on sale (eight ears or more for $1), I'll buy some and boil it (put a teaspoon of sugar in the water just before you add the corn).

For a slightly more impressive barbecue I might marinate and grill some steaks, especially if a good cut of meat is on sale (sirloin or shell steak for less than $1.99 per pound).

For dessert, I always make some kind of pie of whatever fruit is on sale—peaches, strawberries, blueberries, even a delicious blueberry and raspberry pie. However, watermelon is a simple a inexpensive treat that everyone loves, as is a fresh fruit salad. Ice cream sundaes are fun and easy too. They can be surprisingly cheap if you buy the ingredients in bulk—walnuts, chocolate syrup, five-pound tubs of ice cream, whipping cream, and maraschino cherries. Serve each thing in its own dish—not in the container it came in—and reuse leftover ingredients at the next party.

That's our basic barbecue menu for up to thirty people. For smaller groups, we might marinate chicken or steak in vinegar and tarragon or a Terriaki sauce. Almost any oil-and-vinegar-based salad dressing makes a good marinade. Grilled pork chops or sausage (dipped in honey mustard) is wonderful. If tuna steak is on sale, grill it and serve over pasta with olive oil and sautéed garlic. One pound can serve six people this way.

Barbecue season is also the time of year when we make sangria and pitchers of margaritas for our guests. Therefore, I usually have a few bottles of red wine or jugs of store-bought sangria (Carlo Rossi is a great tasting brand, and usually on sale for $5.99 to $7.99 for the four-liter size in the summer) on hand, as well as at least one bottle of the ready-made margarita mix (that is actually cheaper to make than having fresh limes and Triple Sec).

I was invited to a thirtieth birthday party barbecue where the hosts hired a caterer to grill up the food for them (hamburgers, hot dogs, and chicken), because they wanted to make sure they saw guests who had traveled up to one hundred miles for the occasion. While this was a great idea, the caterer was really expensive—and late. I would suggest hiring a local teenager to flip the burgers and preparing some of the food yourself ahead of time. I'd ask various good friends and relatives to make a bowl of potato salad or cole slaw (give them the recipe if they don't have their own), and just serve ice cream or put out a spread of do-it-yourself sundaes in plastic bowls.

A good friend and relative was selling her house, so she decided to have a big Fourth of July barbecue in her backyard. She was afraid no one would come, so she invited everyone she knew (and she worked in a busy store). By the end of the day, she must have had 200 people come and go. She asked everyone to bring something, and she got everything from six-packs of beer to trays of rice and beans. She hired someone to roast a pig on a spit. (Most Latin butchers who sell whole pigs can recommend where to have a spit made. If you're lucky, someone you know grew up in a Latin home and may know how to do this.) She also had burgers and hot dogs grilling on two separate grills. There was a piñata with candy for the kids and a very large store-bought sheet cake. Everyone had a great time, and the barbecue cost her a little over $2 per person.

If you are having a large group (forty or more), you might want to borrow a second grill. If you prefer not to be occupied grilling, hire some neighborhood teenagers to do the cooking so that you'll be free to mingle.

Barbecues are also great for family gatherings when lots of kids are involved. If you can get some summer games for them (horseshoes, hula-hoops, jump rope, even hopscotch or Twister), they should have a good time, and you won't have to worry about them messing up or breaking things in the house.

While there are many themes you can have at a barbecue, the one that goes most easily is a luau. You can serve ribs or pork (or roast a pig), plenty of fruit drinks (with or without the tiny umbrellas), play Hawaiian music in the background, and serve a fruit salad for dessert. You could get your guests to engage in a hula contest and use a broomstick for a limbo contest.

You could do the same thing along a fiesta or tropical theme or try putting together a barbecue along a Wild West theme (this would actually be great for a kids' party).

Picnics

People think of picnics as being very declassé but an elegant picnic is an affair to remember and one that is fairly easy to organize, because you don't have to clean the house.

When I was younger, my standard picnic fare was fried chicken. It wasn't until I was invited to meet some friends for a picnic in Central Park to hear the *1812 Overture* that I learned that a picnic could be so much more. They brought wine and Brie and French bread, sandwiches of salami and more Brie and exotic chicken salads. And grapes. It was delicious, and not much more expensive than the fried chicken I'd brought (maybe even cheaper and certainly easier to make).

Now my husband, son, and I have an annual picnic under the stars in Van Cortlandt Park when there is a free concert, and I pack a picnic basket of wine and Brie, grapes and chicken salad that we all look forward to. Don't forget the blanket when packing for your picnic.

For a more elegant picnic, use matching tablecloths (they can be vinyl) and bring out the crystal. There are wonderful plastic matching plate sets, which run about $20 for an entire set for four, that you can buy at a local department store. A spread of chicken salad tarragon, curried tuna salad, and smoked turkey and Brie served on baguettes or pumpernickel bread, summer fruit, and white wine spritzers will dress up the picnic. Bring a Thermos of coffee and serve iced coffee with a luscious cake—something like cheesecake with strawberries or even a store-bought black forest cake.

Pool Parties

I think of these as outdoor cocktail parties—plenty of snacks and drinks, possibly fruity concoctions like virgin piña coladas.

The food at a pool party should be really light, because people will be going in and out of the water, and you don't want anyone to get sick. I'd recommend lots of pretzels and potato chips, and veggie strips such as carrots, celery, and red and yellow peppers, with a simple sour cream dip made from a soup mix.

If you're serving lunch, make it light too—perhaps a large Caesar salad with grilled chicken or a cobb salad, or simple sandwiches of tuna or chicken salad, or a homemade gazpacho. I wouldn't have a barbecue until evening when people won't be swimming as much.

In the summer, ice cream makes a fantastic dessert. You can get a five-pound tub of Swensen's vanilla ice cream for $5.99 at a wholesale club and dress it up with all sorts of sundae toppings (homemade or store-bought), such as butterscotch, chocolate, or strawberry syrup; sprinkles; M&M's; whipped cream; and cherries). You might also want to make or buy pound cake (they're three for $3.99 at my wholesale club) or angel food cake and serve slices with ice cream and hot sauce or peaches or strawberries.

Garden Parties

The food at a garden party is what you'd serve at an afternoon tea (see chapter 9), but there's a lot you can do with theme and decor if you have a garden in your backyard.

One woman transformed her garden into "fairyland," with classical music playing, scented candles, and floral wreaths as centerpieces. She researched cooking with edible flowers, such as daisies (but make sure they're organically grown, so that you're not feeding your guests pesticides that were never meant to be eaten) and served salads of flowers. This idea can be varied by serving fruits and vegetables presented in a flowerlike way (the radishes and carrots at a good Chinese or Thai restaurant come to mind), but this takes research and is time-consuming to carry out. You could also make daisy chains either as decorations or as a craft activity with your guests.

Another sample theme for a garden party is a more classical one with games such as chess, croquet, and horseshoes. You could even ask guests to come in Victorian costume.

You could also transform the garden into a fairground, with makeshift games (ring toss, pie in the face) and popcorn, cotton candy, Cracker Jacks, and Italian ices—all of which can be bought in bulk.

A well-organized outdoor party on a beautiful summer day can be a truly memorable event for you and your guests. It's usually worth the effort.

9

Odd-Hour Parties

Occasionally, I have found myself in the awkward position of having conflicting entertaining obligations (usually on something like a birthday or Christmas) where I really want to have one side of the family over for "a little something" and am not sure how to put it all together. Sometimes I just want to get a few people together, without slaving away in the kitchen or making a big deal out of it so that they feel they have to return the invitation. These are the times when I put together a mid-morning or early afternoon get-together. Other times I just want people to come by for dessert (usually on a Friday evening, when I've worked all day and cooked dinner for my own family, and only need to straighten up my home before I entertain) or even just come by for a card game.

For these odd-hour get-togethers, you must make it clear what food, if any, will be served, and if there is anything you expect your guests to bring.

Breakfast and Brunch

I serve an annual day-after-Christmas brunch for my cousins who live in Rhode Island. They drive into the city for Christmas Eve, spend Christmas Day with my cousin-in-law's side of the family, and the day after Christmas is the closest we can come to the holiday without causing a scheduling conflict. But I'm exhausted by then (all that shopping and wrapping and cooking and serving), so I don't want to do any more work.

They usually arrive around 11:00 A.M., so the kids have already had a little something to eat. I put out a dozen mixed fresh bagels (you can buy them at a wholesale club where ten bagels sell for $2.79, and bagels freeze very well), some whipped cream cheese, which you can dress up by adding cut up olives, scallions, or sun dried tomatoes, smoked salmon (1½ pounds for $13.99), one sliced purple onion, and a large carton of orange juice and a bottle of Frexiente (a Spanish Cava, which is an excellent champagne for mimosas, for about $5.99 a bottle). There's a fresh pot of coffee with cream and sugar, and perhaps some leftover Greek sweet bread, which we eat with tons of whipped butter. I probably have a fruit pie and some sugar cookies for dessert.

Quiches are a good choice for brunch food: spinach, broccoli, mushroom, salmon, or good old Quiche Lorraine.

You can also offer a plate of fresh fruit (sliced cantaloupe and strawberries are available all year 'round) and cornbread, coffee cake, or a selection of muffins. These baked goods are easy and inexpensive to make with the various mixes on the market or you can buy them cheaply from a wholesale club. Personally, I believe that these are the occasions for which mixes were invented.

If you want to get fancy, you can put out herbed or fruited butter or a selection of doctored-up cream cheeses and jams (homemade, if you're so inclined). You can also add flavoring for the coffee, as well as cinnamon, maple syrup (one of my friends swears by this in her coffee), and powdered chocolate.

It's hard to serve breakfast to a lot of people because it's a chore to keep eggs warm, unless you use warming trays, which I've never been a big fan of. When I have had more than six people for breakfast, I usually make scrambled eggs with cream cheese or huevos rancheros (scrambled eggs, a strip of bacon, and shredded cheddar cheese wrapped in a homemade tortilla and topped with salsa), which I can always warm up in the microwave before serving. However, a Spanish omelette (which is an egg and potato pie) or a fiesta egg scramble (which is really a scrambled egg-casserole) would probably make an equally easy and filling breakfast for many.

My father and husband are great pancake masters, and that is their large breakfast food of choice, but I'm just no good at making them. My dad's favorite was blueberry; I'm partial to chocolate chip. You could also serve waffles (which can be bought in quantity at a wholesale club—forty-eight frozen waffles for $6.99) with fruit (fresh or frozen) and whipped cream.

Sides for breakfast could include either bacon, sausage links, or ham slices (you can try the smoked varieties), all of which you can buy in quantity at a wholesale club (check the two-for-one price at a supermarket on bacon or sliced ham—sometimes our supermarket sells it as a buy-one, get-one-free). The microwave has been a god-send when it comes to cooking quantities of bacon, because it takes so much less time to cook a pound, and you don't have to let it sit in all that bacon fat. Just place four or five pieces on a paper towel on a paper plate and zap for one minute per piece. Sausage or ham, however, is best prepared in a frying pan on the stove.

Homefried potatoes are cheap and easy to make. Boil potatoes the night before, and the next day cut them up and fry them in butter with sliced onions and peppers. Toss on ample paprika for garnish. If you like grits or biscuits and gravy, these are also nice additions to breakfast.

Occasionally, I'll have another mother and her kids over for a breakfast play date. Kids feel like it's a treat if you make them farina or fancy oatmeal (add a teaspoon of vanilla and a dash of cinnamon to the mix).

My son's favorite breakfast is green eggs and ham, which I once brought in to school for his entire class. You add one drop of green food coloring for every three beaten eggs and scramble in melted butter. For the ham, you add one drop of the food coloring to a melted tablespoon of butter, in which you fry all the ham slices. Kids love this! Another green eggs recipe you can try is green deviled eggs; you just add the food coloring to the yolk mixture.

While we don't often think about entertaining for breakfast or brunch, it's actually a great time to get together with other working people, and breakfast and brunch are the most casual of the day's meals, so people don't expect as much. Just make sure the coffee is good and hot, the house is clean and cheerful, and the food is fresh and tasty.

Coffee Clatches

Morning get-togethers are a great time to get see other moms from your kids' school to really find out what's going on (while the kids are in school). Most working moms will take a morning off, or go in to work late, to find out what other parents think of the teacher, the school, or the principal. I find people are a lot more honest (and comfortable) in someone's home than at the PTA meeting. The coffee clatch morning meeting is also a good time to have a committee meeting and, if you host it, it's probably cheaper than going out to breakfast (you can have ten people for less than $10).

Even though these early morning coffees are casual (you invite people by asking them when you drop your kid off to school or with a quick phone call in the early evening), you have to give your guests at least two weeks' warning so that they can rearrange their schedules. Friday mornings seem to be the best time to get together.

The fare at a coffee clatch is very simple—doughnuts, coffee cake, a Danish ring (look for those Dunkin Donut, Sara Lee, or Entenmann's coupons for this), or bagels and cream cheese. You should offer a pot of tea and both caffinated and decaffeinated coffee. If only one person wants decaf, make it fresh brewed using a Melitta funnel.

The decor for a coffee clatch should also be simple—a nice clean tablecloth and a centerpiece of flowers or unlit candles. You can use your good china or silver service for the coffee and tea, but you don't have to.

Afternoon Teas

These can be as casual or as formal as you like—it depends on the occasion and the host.

A baby or engagement shower could be an afternoon tea, in which case it would be much more formal (by written invitation), with matching china teacups and a silver tea service, which you should be able to pick up at a flea market or church bazaar (don't be afraid to negotiate for this). You should also have a lace or linen tablecloth, and you might want to have linen napkins (or at least the fancy beverage napkins). This is the time to use those napkin holders you've been given as presents, or you can make some out of gold foil or thick pastel ribbons (simple is elegant). This is also the time to use those paper doilies under the platters, if they're to your liking.

The food for an afternoon tea can be very simple—from tea sandwiches (white bread, with the crusts removed, stuffed with a selection of egg salad, chicken salad, cucumber and cream cheese or olives, and cream cheese on raisin bread and cut into quarters) to the more elaborate such as scones, ladyfingers, sugar cookies, minicheesecakes, etc.

Make sure you have enough sugar and Nutrasweet, sliced lemons and honey, and put out cream, as well as a low-fat milk. You will probably need more than one sugar and creamer, and you can mix and match these, but try to keep them in the same color scheme. You may also want to put out a few different pots of tea—an Earl Grey, a mint, and perhaps a raspberry. You can put these on the table in teapots of very different patterns—no one will expect you to have matching teapots.

Every year I visit the Jordan Pond Restaurant in Acadia National Park in Bar Harbor, Maine, and have afternoon tea outdoors overlooking a lake. They serve hot popovers with strawberry jam that are out of this world. For a group of twelve or less, popovers are wonderful, and easy to make. You just have to refrigerate the batter the night before and bake them in muffin pans.

If you're having a very formal tea, where you really want to impress or entertain your guests, you might want to hire a teenage girl to pour the tea and serve the tea sandwiches. She should wear a dress and an apron, and you could ask her to wear gloves for a special effect.

Dessert Parties

I like having people over for dessert, usually around 7:00 P.M. if there are children coming.

As with breakfast and coffee clatches, I make sure everyone knows I'm just serving coffee and dessert. If it's a workday, I might ask each family to bring something. This way I have more variety to offer.

As usual, I like to make a pie, (typically apple, because I buy bags of Macintosh and Granny Smith apples on a regular basis, so I always have some on hand) and cookies or brownies. I would make both coffee and tea.

If I was feeling particularly festive, I might buy some coffee flavorings (hazelnut, chocolate raspberry, vanilla—although you can make them yourself, if you have time) or buy one or two of those creamers with flavor (Irish creme, amaretto, French vanilla). I might also put out a selection of after-dinner cordials (we always stock Bailey's Irish Creme, Kahlua, and Cointreau) to add to the coffee, as well as whipped cream. Cinnamon sticks or chocolate-covered candy stirrers (two boxes for $8 at Costco—they make great gifts too) add a nice touch.

One of my husband's cousins makes a wonderful flan (a Latin custard) which she often brings. Crème brûlée is a nice offering at this sort of event. Rice pudding also goes extremely well this time of year, as does a homemade trifle (a sort of kitchen-sink dessert that's great when you have a little bit of everything left over). I also found a recipe for a sort-of homemade ice cream cake (a layer of mashed graham crackers, Kahlua and rum, coffee ice cream, mashed up macaroons, chocolate shavings, and frozen whipped cream) that's very fancy and impressive, and easy, so I might serve that. It takes about twenty minutes to prepare, but you have to freeze it for two hours.

You can make your dessert gathering even fancier if you have a cappuccino machine, or you might borrow a neighbor's. While expensive and fancy espresso is the rage, it's easy to make with a Greca, which is a stainless-steel two-piece coffeepot you heat on the stove that sells for about $8 to $10 in neighborhood hardware stores and up to $40 in department stores. My mother-in-law makes espresso by straining hot coffee through a cheesecloth sock that she washes out. Lots of sugar and a lemon peel are nice touches with espresso. You might be able to pick up a set of demitasse cups cheaply at a rummage sale or buy a set for about $10 at a housewares outlet.

Card Games

I used to be in a weekly poker game that started around 8:00 P.M. and ended around 11:30. Many of the people came after work and were supposed to have eaten, but hadn't, so the snacks we had were important. We took a contribution from each player of something like $5 each, but the person who was hosting was supposed to have the food and beverages there when we arrived (about $20 to $25 worth).

Each host was also responsible for poker chips (at least 200 for five players) and cards, which cost a bundle if you have to run out and buy them at the last minute, but which can be found at any dollar store if you plan ahead (sometimes you can get two decks of cards for a dollar).

When the guys hosted, we usually just had the old potato chips, canned dip, pretzels, peanuts, and beer fare. However, they loved it when I would put out a bowl of guacamole, microwaved popcorn, a soup mix dip with veggie sticks, and, if I was feeling particularly creative, a batch of microwaved nachos (so cheap and easy). A box of frozen appetizers from a wholesale club (jalapeño poppers for instance) will run about $7 for forty, and they're a big hit. The more traditional appetizers like pigs in a blanket go over well here too. They are certainly cheaper to make if you have the time, but our poker games were always on a weeknight, so I had to go for the ready-made.

To stretch the dollar on the drinks, I often made a pitcher of iced tea instead of serving soda (everyone seems to like it). Beer is a staple at these games, so I usually have two six-packs. I always make sure I empty my ice trays into a large bowl in the freezer and refill them before the players arrive.

Odd-hour parties can be a challenge, but they can also be fun and warm in a more casual way than the full-scale luncheons and dinners.

10

Children's Birthday Parties

Anyone who has ever thrown a few kids' parties, or gone to a few hundred parties for kids, and has more than one child in their family, knows how expensive these parties can be—and how important they are to your child.

I truly admire Amy Dacyczyn for throwing her son a pirate party, described in the first volume of *The Tightwad Gazette* (Villard Books, 1992) for something like $10. It's inspiring to know it can be done! While I don't think I'll ever manage to get away that cheaply, I made a personal vow that my son's birthday parties would not be more expensive than a family weekend in Washington, D.C. With a lot of thought and ingenuity and hard work, I've managed to throw better kids' parties and save myself a bundle.

Kids' parties break down into a couple of categories—at home (indoors or outdoors), in a rented space, or at an entertainment facility. They also break down into age groups because you can't throw the same kind of party for a toddler as for a teenager.

The Basic At-Home Kids' Party

If you're having a kids' party at home, whether the child is three or thirteen, there is a basic shape to the party. You should have between six and twenty kid guests (more than that will be hard to accommodate indoors), usually for lunch, but sometimes for an early dinner. Friday evenings seem to be more and more popular for kids' parties these days.

The meal should be kid-friendly and can be anything from hot dogs, pizza, or chicken tenders to peanut butter and jelly sandwiches. If you are making a barbecue, kids love burgers, ribs, or chicken. Fried mozzarella sticks with marinara sauce are a nice treat, and you can buy them in bulk at a wholesale club—fifty sticks for $6.99.

It's tempting to go with juice boxes for drinks because they're easy, but they'll run you about $7 for thirty. Better to buy jugs of juice and soda or make lemonade, iced tea, or root beer floats, which are favorites from my childhood. I like to serve egg creams and milk-shakes, and ice cream sodas which are terrific kid pleasers.

The choice of cake should be up to your child: an ice cream cake; a themed sheet cake from a bakery; a special themed cake with a homemade filling or frosting; cupcakes, which the kids can decorate themselves; or ice cream sundaes.

You should have balloons around the house, as well as streamers, and *Happy Birthday* signs and murals, which can be homemade. You can even have the guests help decorate a commemorative mural, using a white tablecloth or packing paper taped to the wall and asking each guest to contribute.

For a young child, hats and a birthday tablecloth on the table are de rigueur. I like to have themed tableware, but you could use just plain paper cups, plates, and napkins. You could also have the kids make their own hats out of newspaper or construction paper.

Children's birthday parties last between two and three hours. You need some sort of entertainment, whether it's party games with prizes (the old standards are pin the tail on the donkey, musical chairs, hot potato, pass the parcel, charades, bean toss, etc.), a movie, watching a sporting event (for slightly older kids), paid entertainment, arts and crafts, dancing, karaoke, or limbo. Girls sometimes have makeover parties, at home or at a beauty parlor.

I love piñatas, for children of all ages. You can vary what you fill it with for the different ages of the children, but all kids love bashing at a swaying target and then diving for candies and prizes.

For a birthday child under ten, I believe in goodie bags for the guests. Many kids open their presents in front of their guests, and it's hard for a kid not to feel a little jealous. Goodie bags take the sting out. You don't have to fill it with outrageously expensive things, just candy and snacks and a few choice items from the dollar store.

While a kid's party *can* cost as little as $10, that's not realistic for me with my working, urban life. I'd say $100 is a good, average budget for a themed kids' party in my house for twenty kids (including coffee and cake for any adults who want to hang around). A hundred-dollar budget makes me feel like I can be creative, but without overspending. It's also about what I budget for most of my at-home adult parties, so I feel like I truly am treating my son like any other member of the family. A comparative party would run me at least $300 at a children's entertainment facility, so I know I'm way ahead of the game.

About three months before my son's birthday, I start casing the dollar stores, Odd Lots, Webers, and party outlet stores to see what themes are on sale (I have a friend who spent $80 on party decorations and tableware alone). I then begin presenting my son with his options for this year's party theme (usually about four). Kids tend to have fairly basic theme ideas, so it's not hard to match up your child's wishes with what you can afford, or to make him think it was *his* idea to have a Flubber party (all that green Jell-o and green drinks) when you thought of it because you saw the Flubber stuff for 50 percent off.

Once your kid has chosen a theme, you can go through all the party elements (hats, tableware, goodie bags, games or entertainment, music, food, cake) and see how you can tailor each one to the theme. Some of the themes might have websites where you can go for ideas (such as Disney and Seussville), and some might even have forums where you can get feedback from other parents and kids.

Kids' party invitations can be store-bought to go with the theme, but they are expensive this way, especially if you're inviting the child's whole class as well as relatives. You can just as easily make something up on the computer. Your child can help design or write the invitations.

You *must* send out thank-you notes to those who attended, as well as those who sent a gift without coming. You should sit down with your child and write these together (or have him write them, if he is old enough). This is an important lesson, and should be taught young. You should send the thank-yous out no later than ten days after the party. These too can be homemade and are actually sweeter if they're designed and written by the child.

How to Make a Piñata

Sometimes, if you're really lucky, a piñata that goes with your child's theme or a generic birthday piñata (rainbow, birthday cake) is on super sale (less than $5, although I've actually bought these for $1). If you live near the Mexican border you might be able to get one really cheap in a border town. However, it's just as easy to make them, and a lot more fun for your child.

A piñata is easy to make, but you have to start it a few days before you need it. Blow up a balloon (this will give you a circular or tubular shape to start with) and cover it with newspaper strips generously dipped in a paste made of equal amounts (usually about 2½ cups each) of flour and water. For the average piñata, you'll need between twenty and thirty one-inch wide strips of newspaper. To make a figure, add empty toilet paper and paper towel rolls for arms and legs or necks and beaks. Attach them to the balloon with masking tape, then cover with the newspaper strips. Finish shaping the piñata to your heart's desire. Let the piñata dry overnight, and pop the balloon with a pin. The empty space is where the candy and prizes go.

Paint the outside of the piñata with acrylic paint (you can pick up the four primary colors for $1, so don't bother mixing paint together for this) and decorate. Let the paint dry overnight. Add extras to the piñata the next day, such as tissue paper, glitter, buttons, etc. Also attach a bobby pin or paper clip somewhere on the piñata, so you have a place to tie the string when you hang it. You also have to carve a small circular hole in the back of the piñata through which you can add the candy. You can tape the hole up again when the pinata is full.

The easiest piñatas to make are the superheros (capes made out of tissue paper, which you can also pick up at the dollar store), Mickey Mouse's head, animals, dinosaurs and dinosaur eggs, etc. Use your imagination, and you should be able to come up with a simplified version of the piñata of your child's dreams using basic shapes (circular torsos made from balloons, arms and legs from paper rolls, beaks and necks from rolled up cardboard, oak tag, or construction paper).

If your kid insists on a difficult piñata (a castle, a pirate ship) and you can't talk him into a simpler one associated with the theme (a knight, a pirate chest), then you may have to buy one. They run anywhere from $10 to $25 at a party store or Toys 'R Us.

Filling the piñata is easy too. Buy dollar-store bags of individually wrapped candy and gum, such as Bazooka, mini peanut-butter cups, mini Life Saver packs, chocolate bars, Tootsie rolls, and lollipops, as well as a few more impressive items such as ring pops, wax lips (a personal favorite), giant Sweet-tarts, whistles, erasers, candy necklaces, small cars, etc. Most party and dollar stores have a party section where they offer packages of six or eight prizes for a dollar. This is definitely where you should be looking for piñata filling, although I have seen a bag of candy and treats sold as piñata filling for about $5 (this is a bargain, if you can find it). If you have odd pieces left over from the goodie bags, put them in here too.

Use a child's baseball bat or a broomstick to swat the piñata. If you have really young kids, you might have to "start" the opening, but do that after each child has taken a turn.

Making Up Goodie Bags

Unless you run yourself ragged, these will cost you a minimum of $1 per bag. Some people can do it for less, but I would lose my mind trying.

You do not have to buy fancy goodie bags. Most kids are so anxious to see what's inside, they don't even notice that you went to the trouble of getting *Star Wars* bags (which run something like eight for $2.99). Of course, if they're on sale, and absolutely precious, you might consider it, but it's more for you than for the kids.

It is easy to make your own party bags. Use either brown lunch bags (fifty for $1) or white bakery bags (you might ask the local bakery if you can buy twenty-five for $1—they'll probably give them to you for free) and do some simple art on the bags to go with the party. It could be as simple as writing "Happy Birthday" or "Goodie Bag" in glitter on the bags. One woman hosted a *101 Dalmatians* party and bought a rubber stamp of dog paw prints, which she stamped on brown bags. You can buy stickers of the theme and plaster them on the bags or stencil the bags with pictures related to the theme. Simple and easy is the key.

You could do more impressive things like find thermal lunch bags at a dollar store (I've seen them on sale at the end of the school year) and write each child's name in glitter glue on the outside of the lunch bag. The bag then becomes part of the goodies, and you fill it up with a sample school lunch (juice box, raisins, apple, Rice Crispies treats, Fruit by the Foot). My son was invited to a party where this was done, and I was impressed.

You can also have goodie bags along seasonal themes such as back to school, Halloween, Christmas, and summer vacation.

The back-to-school goodie bags featured school carry-cases with pencils, erasers, pencil sharpeners, rulers, and notepads. You can get these at a dollar store. The case is the goodie bag.

For Halloween, you can make a white bag into a ghost or buy trick-or-treat bags (which should be fairly inexpensive) and use these. You should be able to buy such things as bat or ant rings, eyeball chocolates, Halloween magnets, wax lips with fangs, face painting kits, fangs, fake fingertips, press-on tattoos, and plastic bugs and snakes to put in the bags.

For Christmas, you could wrap a ribbon around the bag so that it looks like a present or make your own bags out of cheap wrapping paper ($1 a roll). You could put in Christmas magnets, red-and-green foil-covered chocolates, and candy canes. You can have the kids make ornaments at the party (see chapter 6), and use these as part of the goodie bag as well.

Summer goodie bags include bottles of bubbles, sidewalk chalk, shovels, sand molds, and water guns. Kids love these.

I put about four items in each goodie bag, and about four pieces of candy and/or snack food, unless I give each kid one big present.

Miscellaneous items for goodie bags, many of which can be purchased in packs of six or eight or ordered in bulk from a party or teacher catalog, are: whistles, stickers, tattoos, crayon packs, bubbles, chalk, erasers, water guns, whoopie cushions and other gag novelties, mini puzzles, watercolor paint kits, pencils, decorative pens, Magic Markers, clay, Silly Putty, slinkies, bouncing balls, click-clacks, paddles with balls, jacks, cars, fake makeup for girls, lip gloss, berets, kid sunglasses, kid disguise glasses, imitation Beanie Babies and teddy bears, etc.

I don't like to fill the goodie bags with candy, because as a mother, I don't like my son to come home all excited from a party and then bounce off the walls for a few hours from all the candy he's eaten. I usually include one or two pieces of candy, a Toosie pop, some gum, and then snack foods like fruit roll-ups, bags of peanuts, Rice Crispies treats, raisins, etc.

One woman found a store where they had kids' jigsaw puzzles for a dollar. She gave each kid his choice of a puzzle (they were Disney puzzles) and skipped the bags entirely. Another mom bought action figures at deep discount and gave them out to each kid without the bag.

Another mom waited until she knew exactly who was coming (she sent the invitations out very early) and ordered individual stampers with each kid's name on it from Lillian Vernon. She added stamp pads and some treats, and the bags ran her about $3 per kid. This was quite thoughtful and creative.

Kids' Games

We all assume that everyone knows the standard children's games, but there are always one or two that are unfamiliar to someone. For instance, I never played Pass the Parcel at parties when I was a kid.

Since game are competitive, you might want to have small gifts for the kids who win. They should be different from what you put in the goodie bags. I usually buy three or four special toys at the dollar store, such as a puzzle, action toy, or Barbie-type doll clothing for the girls.

Musical Chairs. Count the number of kids and have one chair less than that number. Arrange the chairs in a line or circle, and place a kid in front of each chair. Leave a space for the chair that is "missing." When the kids are in place, play music (a cassette player is best for this) and have the kids walk around in the circle or around the line of chairs. When the music is stopped, the kids scramble for seats. The kid left without a seat loses that round, and a chair is removed.

You do this until there is only one chair and two kids left. The kid sitting in the chair at the end wins the round.

Hot Potato.   This has the same concept as musical chairs. The kids sit in a circle and pass a ball (one mother actually used a potato wrapped in aluminum foil) around the circle (pretending it's hot) accompanied by music. When the music stops abruptly, whoever is holding the ball loses that round. The last kid left without the ball wins.

Pass the Parcel.   This concept is similar to Hot Potato, but with a twist. The kids sit in a circle and a gift-wrapped box is passed around. When the music stops, whoever is holding the parcel unwraps one layer. There's usually four or five layers of wrapping, so the kid unwrapping the present on the sixth stop gets to keep the present inside. You can do this a couple of times.

Pin the Tail on the Donkey.   A drawing of a donkey (or any other animal you want or some person or creature that goes with your birthday theme) is taped to a wall. Each kid is given a tail with tape, blindfolded, spun around a couple of times so that he loses his bearings, and then let loose to hopefully pin the tail on the donkey. However, the kids are usually way off base and end up pinning the tail on the donkey's nose or knees, which makes for lots of laughs. The kid whose tail lands closest to where the tail is supposed to be wins this game.

Bean Toss.   Using a cardboard box, you make a target of some sort (usually pretty big and round, so the kids have a chance of getting it in) and give them three to five bean bags that they toss at the target. The kid who gets the most bull's-eyes wins.

Charades.   This is for slightly older kids (five and up) because they have to work as a team. Divide the kids into teams of three, four, or five and have them pick clues that you've made up ahead of time related to movies, books, characters a kid would know, or to the theme of the party.

One kid on each team picks a clue from a bowl or hat and has two or three minutes (use a timer) to pantomime it for the other kids on his team so that they guess what it is. If the time runs out before they guess correctly, they lose the round and the other teams can guess at the clue. Whichever team has the most correct answers wins, and you give prizes to all the team members.

Pictionary. For Pictionary, you need an easel with large paper on which the kids draw clues for their teammates. They pick a clue out of a hat and then must illustrate the clue, either as a word or in syllables, in a given time.

This is by no means a complete list of games to play at kids' parties, but these are the most common ones. You can also have a treasure hunt, which involves hiding items around the house or backyard. A limbo contest can be lots of fun, but you have to find a way to set up a broom horizontally about four feet off the ground and then be able to lower it little by little. Kids have to walk under the broom without touching it or be disqualified. The broom is lowered slightly after each round. The last child standing is the winner. Another game is to have all the kids try to keep a balloon up in the air by batting it around volleyball-style. Whoever lets the balloon touch the ground is out.

Themes for Parties

Creating a well-thought-out theme party is easy, it just takes time and creativity. The goal of a child's birthday party should be to make a child's fantasies come true for a day.

Choose a theme for your child's party based on his or her favorite movies, TV shows, and hobbies. Before you approach your child with your ideas, give each one a little thought yourself, so you have some basic ideas on how you would put it together.

Indiana Jones. This year we threw an Indiana Jones party. We sent out photocopied black-and-white invitations picturing Harrison Ford in his Dr. Jones gear, inviting my son's friends to a reception to honor Dr. Jones after his return from the Amazon.

We decided to re-create the banquet in *Indiana Jones and the Temple of Doom,* which consisted of eyeball soup, rhino beetles, snake surprise, and chilled monkey brains. I made tomato soup with floating Ping Pong balls for eyeballs (7 cents each at my local party store), which was a big hit with the kids, and they each got to take Ping Pong balls home. I found plastic rhino beetles at the party store

(13 cents each) and put one on each slice of pizza I served the kids. I photocopied a simple drawing of a monkey's head and glued it to the outside of a paper cup and served orange and raspberry sherbet as the chilled monkey brains. A homemade chocolate cake with candy worms and snakes arranged to spell out "Happy Birthday" was the snake surprise.

For the activities, we has a treasure hunt in the park outside our building. The treasure was a plastic Ferraro chocolate box crammed with fake coins and dollar bills, necklaces, rings, and charms. We made a map of the park and gave each kid a piece of it, which they had to put together to find the treasure. We also glued or taped plastic spiders, bugs, snakes, and mice on to playground equipment, and the kids put these in their goodie bags when they found them.

After the treasure hunt, we had them smack a spider piñata, which I was lucky enough to find for $10. I filled it with skull and bat rings, candy necklaces, and candy that I bought in a variety pack.

I was also lucky enough to find plastic "gangster" hats (fedoras) in the party store for 79 cents each. The found candy and plastic bugs and the hat were the kids' party favors.

I had intended to use a plain white paper tablecloth with a hand-drawn treasure map as the table covering, but I was really lucky to find a set of tableware with an insect motif at 50 percent off at the local party store. The tablecloth was plastic, which was an added bonus.

Princess.   This is a universal party theme for girls, ages three to twelve.

One mother created a princess party by buying a whole bunch of party and prom dresses at rummage sales before her daughter's birthday. She let the girls add glitter and sequins and jeweled buttons and sashes. She also bought a ton of rummage sale costume jewelry for them to wear. Princess hats were made out of oak tag covered with material with a rummage-sale scarf thrust through the hole in the top to hang down the back.

Lunch was an elegant tea party with sandwiches and cake. You could also feature a light fare such as quiche or crepes.

Better than any goodie bag, each girl got to take home her princess costume. If you still wanted to include a goodie bag though, great choices would be generic necklaces, rings, makeup, fake nails, tiaras, and glass slippers (which I found at a party store for 34 cents each).

Medieval Times. The first thing I would do is re-create the meal they serve at the Medieval Times restaurant—garlic bread, a vegetable soup that's drunk out of a bowl, chicken, ribs, and roasted potatoes eaten with the hands (which kids love). I'd serve soda or cider in plastic beer mugs, and cupcakes, which are easily eaten with the hands.

Each kid would make his own knight tunic (just precut felt and hot glue), as well as his own coat of arms on a shield (white oak tag on cardboard with a strap glued on). If there were going to be a few girls, I might have them work on a princess dress as described in the princess party section.

For games, I might have an archery contest of some sort, with rubber stick-on arrows, and some variation of Hot Potato (Hot Grail), and musical chairs with Gregorian chants. Maybe a Pin the Tail on the Horse or Pin the Horn on the Unicorn or Pin the Fire on the Dragon.

I would want to give each boy a plastic sword or axe with his goodie bag, but I'd ask the moms first. Some moms are dead set against their children having weapons, and I wouldn't want to make anyone uncomfortable.

Pirate. As I said, I was so impressed with Amy Dacyczyn's brilliant pirate party in the first volume of *The Tightwad Gazette,* and that's as cheap as it gets. She built a pirate ship in a barn out of old sheets and odds and ends. The kids also had a treasure hunt with clues that led to a treasure box with 300 chocolate-covered coins, which the kids split as their goodie bag loot.

The food consisted of generic soda and ice cream, and a sheet cake with a treasure map on it. Dacyczyn says that the party cost less than $10. However, this is clearly the kind of party that requires a basement or backyard (or a rental space).

An indoor party can be done by making pirate costumes for all the kids (eye patches, bandannas, pirate hats—black felt or newspaper hats). Maybe let the kids make their own pirate flags. The treasure hunt with chocolate coins is the perfect activity for a pirate party, whether it's indoors or out. I might have the kids make their own swords out of two crossed pieces of cardboard or wood or I might supply plastic swords in the goodie bags.

The pirate party theme can be easily adapted into a *Peter Pan* party, if that is one of your child's favorite films or stories.

Movie Star.   You'll need lots of rummage-sale clothing (men's suits and gowns), lots of makeup and hair styling items, and lots of sunglasses, feather boas, wild hats, glittery jewelry.

One mother put up a sheet on a wall and took pictures of all the kids in their movie star getups. She had multiple prints made of the pictures, and then gave the guests picture books as their memento from the party.

If you know of a shop that sells old magazines, try to negotiate a good price on some back issues of old movie-star magazines, and give them out as souvenirs.

You can make placemats out of cutouts from current magazines (lots of pictures of Leonardo) or you could draw a "Hollywood star" out of glitter at each place setting and write the guest's name in.

You could do a similar theme with the sheet cake. Using white frosting as the base, make a large star in the center with the birthday child's name, and then draw smaller stars with the guests' names around it in another color frosting. The kids will be tickled.

Dinosaur.   This kind of party is a big favorite for younger kids. You can call it a *Land Before Time* party or just a dinosaur dig.

Kids love a dinosaur dig, which you can have in the backyard (you can buy bones or make your own fossils with plaster of paris molds or just make a bone mold). You could also have a dinosaur egg hunt, using those plastic Easter eggs (put a tiny plastic dinosaur inside each egg). You can also play Hot Dinosaur Egg, a variation on the Hot Potato game.

For the cake, you could make that exploding volcano cake featured on TV (look the recipe up on the Internet using a search engine for "volcano cake" or through the library) and put plastic dinosaurs on the icing.

There are lots of arts and crafts possibilities with this theme. You can tape white paper to the walls and ask the kids to draw or paint a mural like the ones they've seen in the museums. We bought dinosaur molds at a natural history museum. If you make dinosaurs from the plaster of paris molds, the kids can paint them at the party and take the painted dinosaurs home as souvenirs.

For the tablecloth, you could put each kid's place setting in a giant dinosaur footprint. A dinosaur piñata would be easy to make (most likely candidates are brontosaurus and stegosaurus) and easy to fill. Same for the goodie bags, which you could make out of brown paper bags with dinosaur footprints stamped on and filled with plastic dinosaurs, dinosaur stickers, chocolate covered "dinosaur eggs," etc.

Goosebumps/Haunted House. It seems that everywhere I turn, I can find Goosebumps stuff on sale for a fraction of the cost, which is why I suggest a Goosebumps party.

The great thing about a Goosebump party is that it's really a Halloween party. Encourage the kids to come in costumes. You could serve a witch's brew. The cake could be decorated to look like a graveyard.

Party games could be a blast: dunk for apples; turn your home into a haunted house with cobwebs and funny scary gags throughout (look up "Halloween decorations" in your local library). Blindfold the kids and have them place their hands in bowls or boxes filled with stuff that will gross them out . . . but thrill them through and through! Have them put their hands in a bowl of water and spaghetti and tell them it's brains; have them hold a peeled, very lightly boiled egg, which you tell them is an eyeball; and put some wet dough in a plastic bag and tell them it's someone's liver. Kids love this kind of stuff! Don't forget to play scary music you can buy on Halloween CD's.

Since I'm pretty well-stocked with Halloween decorations, I would probably use my Halloween tablecloth, cookie jar, candlesticks, etc. For a meal in winter, I might make pumpkin beef stew (beef stew served inside a jack-o'-lantern) or jack-o'-lantern shaped pasta.

For goodie bags, in addition to all the fangs and spiders you could put in the bags, as well as Goosebumps pencils and rulers, you can buy the Goosebumps books fairly cheaply from Scholastic or sometimes you can get four- or five-book sets at Costco.

Superheroes. This is a fairly easy party to put together because most of the items you need can be bought inexpensively. I've had three superhero parties, and for every one I was able to get tableware for at least 50 percent off. It's easy to make a sheet cake and decorate it with the superhero's insignia (Batman's or Superman's) or just buy little superhero figurines and put them in the icing. You're also likely to find a superhero piñata for a good price, although they are easy to make (see the piñata section of this chapter).

I tried to find corresponding comic books for the goodie bags (four for $1 at the dollar store or you might be able to bargain for old comics at the local comic book store—they usually have plenty of old comics they just can't sell). Other trinkets in the goodie bag may include stickers and a fruit roll candy with the superhero embossed on it. You might get lucky and find a superhero video for a dollar.

If you are extremely generous and handy with a sewing machine, you could easily whip up a half dozen or so capes (with cotton material from a discount store, felt insignia). The kids would love you forever.

Space/Aliens.   Astronauts and aliens are favorite kid fantasies right now, so it should be pretty easy to put together a space/aliens party. The piñata could be in the shape of a space craft or a planet or an alien head, filled with little NASA-like figurines (they sell them in packages like toy soldiers now), alien erasers, alien lollipops, "moon" rocks, etc.

You can decorate the house with the solar system, either homemade cutouts or mini-piñata planets. NASA will send you packets of information and posters free (or for the cost of postage) if you write or E-mail them, and you could put some of these in the goodie bags and use others as decorations. You can play Pin the Planet on the Solar System, Hot Sun, Planet Toss, etc.

You can serve Tang with the birthday lunch. You can also buy space ice cream or a cake in the shape of a spacecraft, or decorate a sheet cake with the solar system.

Arts and Crafts.   This is for kids who love to create things. You can do anything from ceramic molds (premade) to tie-dying and T-shirt decorating (with glitter glue or special T-shirt paint), as well as making ornaments for Christmas.

For boys, you can make models, using store-bought kits for cars, boats, and body parts to ships in bottles, wooden airplanes, and even

Legos. You'd be surprised at how cheaply you can buy some of these (as little as a dollar or two per child).

For girls, beading parties are always a success, as are other jewelry-making gatherings. You can buy everything inexpensively at a craft store, or you can make the beads out of baked clay or rolled-up magazines. Look at back issues of craft and women's magazines for ideas, and visit craft sites on the Internet.

In general, though, you have to be extremely well prepared for these kind of parties with kids (picture glue in the hair and paint on your rugs and floor), but they can be a lot of fun, especially when the kid has a memento he's made by himself to remind him of the party.

You can easily fill goodie bags with art supplies for under a dollar. I've seen watercolor sets, pastels, glitter glue, packages of paint brushes, and all sorts of art supplies for sale in bulk at dollar stores. You can also buy a lot of this stuff at art stores and through craft catalogs or general merchandise catalogs (see Resources for a list of suggested catalogs).

Alice in Wonderland/Through the Looking Glass. A friend of mine turned her living room into Alice's Wonderland for her daughter's sixth birthday. She copied the illustrations from the Tenniel edition of the book, had a Mad Tea Party lunch, played indoor croquet, and had the girls make houses of cards. For the goodie bag, she gave out little porcelain tea sets that she picked up at the dollar store, mini-editions of the book, and a deck of cards so the girls could make their own house of cards at home.

Dr. Seuss. A Dr. Seuss party is great for young kids, ages three to six. The Children's Museum of Manhattan (www.CMOM.org) is in the midst of running a two-year tribute to the author, through the fall of 1999, and has transformed a floor of the museum into an indoor Seuss playground, so many of the ideas I've come up with have been inspired by what they've done on a larger scale. Also, there is a Dr. Seuss Web site (www.Seussville), which has a wealth of games and ideas for you.

There's a lot you can do with the Cat in the Hat motif, such as hiding a number of pink dots (made out of felt or construction paper) throughout the home for the kids to find and "clean," like in *The Cat in the Hat Comes Back,* with brooms and feather dusters. You can also have each child make a Cat in the Hat hat for himself (oak tag stovepipe hats) that you let the kids decorate themselves. You can draw Seuss-like animals from *There's a Wocket in My Pocket* and place them in the spots that Seuss put them (the Zink in the sink and the Zelf on the shelf). The kid who finds the most Seuss characters gets a prize.

Kids can also make Seuss animals (like those crazy made-up ones in *If I Ran the Zoo* or *One Fish, Two Fish* and *There's a Wocket in My Pocket*) out of empty bottles and egg cartons, and put them on display with the funny names that the kids came up with. The kids could make Seuss fish out of painted and stuffed newspaper (stapled together) and then hang them from hangers for a *One Fish, Two Fish* mobile. The kids could "fish" for Seuss fish in a bucket or plastic pool with a magnet and paper clips, and the one with the most fish wins a prize. You can make all your own decorations and party favors, because that's in keeping with the spirit of the party.

The cake can either be a Cat in the Hat–shaped hat or a sheet cake decorated to look like the cover of your child's favorite Seuss book. You can serve strawberry-flavored Quick with straws as the pink ink that the Yink drinks. A Seuss party can be a blast.

Winnie the Pooh.   The same friend of mine who transformed her house into Wonderland also, on the occasion of her four-year-old daughter's birthday, turned the house into the 100 Acre Wood. She made her own Winnie the Pooh decorations for the walls (Rabbit's House in one corner, Owl's in another, etc.) and made newspaper hats for the kids (à la Christopher Robin). For party games she hid real carrots throughout the apartment (with their greens) and the kid who found the most carrots won a prize, which was somehow Pooh-related, such as stickers or pens. There was a Pooh cake and Pooh-related stuff in the goodie bags.

Disney movies tend to have a lot of tie-in opportunities, so definitely visit the Web site for ideas (www.disney) for games and recipes. You can do the same for almost any popular children's movie or TV show. Try the Web sites at www.nick.com, kidsWarnerbros.com, dccomics.com, marvel.com and barbie.com, just to name a few.

Teen Parties and Slumber Parties

When kids get a little older, they sometimes get more demanding, and a generic birthday party is often just not enough. A little ingenuity can go a long way here.

It's a lot easier to have house parties for teenage girls, but you can come up with creative parties for boys, if you try. Sports events, movies, or arcades are some obvious choices.

Some girls like makeup or manicure parties or hair styling parties. If you have a friend who is particularly good at this, now's the time to ask for a favor.

One family served the daughter's friends a fancy five-course meal chosen by the daughter. The mom and dad dressed up as a chef and a maître d' for the night.

You could also have a number of girls over for a cooking party. Let the birthday girl pick out the menu. Each guest could receive photocopied recipes and photos of them cooking as a memento.

When kids are older, the meal can also be much easier because they know exactly what they want. You can order in Chinese food with fortune cookies or Japanese sushi. It's up to you and your child.

If the girls are creative, you might want to have a jean skirt– or jean bag–making party. We used to do these all the time when I was a teenager. We would make maxiskirts from old jeans and sew in triangles of bandanna, tapestry, or velvet material between the pants' legs. We'd also make miniskirts as well as shoulder bags out of the jeans. You might want to tie-dye material to be sewn between the pants' legs, so that all the skirts are the same, and add a batch of matching T-shirts.

You can easily make any of these teen parties into a slumber party (have the girls bring sleeping bags or make bed rolls), keeping the number of guests to six or seven. In addition to a crafts or makeup session, rent videos for the girls and serve them an exotic breakfast in the morning or take them out to breakfast.

Mad Libs are great fun at these parties. You fill in the blanks of a poem, story, or essay, so that it comes out funny—"Four Score and seven _____ ago," etc. They still sell these, but you can easily make some for the party.

Truth or Dare, where you ask each other embarrassing questions and chose whether to answer or take a dare, is still a popular way for girls to have some good laughs together. They might also want to play Magic Eight Ball (which you can pick up in novelty stores—look for the kind of store that would sell lava lamps), where you ask this supposedly magic ball questions, usually about boys, and it answers yes, no, or maybe.

When I was twelve or so, we started playing with Ouija boards and Tarot cards. If you are so inclined, you might consider dressing up as a fortune teller and reading the girls' fortunes. *It's All in the Cards* by Chita St. Lawrence (just published by Perigee Books) instructs you on how to tell fortunes with regular playing cards.

Renting Space

Renting space will add $50 to $100 to your party budget, but it will ease your mind for clean-up and survival of your rugs, walls, and furniture. If you're having more than twenty kids and their parents, and you don't have a backyard or a big house, you might want to consider this, especially because the space will come with parking.

As I mentioned in chapter 4, you can usually find space to rent in a co-op or condo building, the local community center, or even a health club (one little girl's parents had an exercise party there, complete with trainer). You might also want to consider renting space if you are going to be having a particularly messy arts and crafts party or food-related event, or if your party theme will have a number of big games (such as a circus or carnival theme).

Many parents hold their party at a children's entertainment facility, such as Discovery Zone, or a kid-oriented restaurant like Chuck E Cheese's and the fast food chains, but they're all expensive and not very personal. This isn't really entertaining, since you're not throwing the party.

Birthday Entertainment and Help

If you decide to have a home or rented-room party, and want to supply the entertainment, there are a number of options. On average, they will run you an additional $50 to $100.

A great source for entertainment is the local community center, where your child might already be taking classes with a teacher who might be interested in supplying a half hour to an hour's worth of instruction or entertainment for a bunch of kids. These usually include people who teach music or art to youngsters (we have a Musical Munchkins woman who teaches kids songs, plays guitar, and brings a bag of triangles, maracas, and tambourines for the kids to play along). The art teacher could guide the kids in making birthday hats or mementos. If you have a backyard, or access to a gym, the local coach might be persuaded into giving young boys basic tips on basketball, soccer, or baseball, depending on the time of year.

Traditional staples of at-home entertainment include clowns and magicians, but one variation on this theme is to have the clown or the magician teach the kids how to do the tricks or pratfalls. Kids would remember this more than the average party. You could then put sample tricks or gags in their goodie bags.

You could also have a good friend come by and paint the kids' faces or do it yourself (I've seen some wonderful designs for super-hero face painting). A beautician could be hired to do manicures for girls or set their hair (call beauty schools for this) or do beauty makeovers. You can then give out makeup and nail polish or hair products in the goodie bags.

If you are planning a complicated craft project for young kids such as glitter-glue T-shirts for five-year-olds, you might want to hire a teenager to act as an extra set of party hands. You could probably also use the help in getting the food from the kitchen to the kids and back again, if you're having a large number of kids and their parents don't stay. They'll also help with cleaning up after the party is over.

I pay my teenage help at least $5 an hour but I know that teenagers are often paid less outside of cities.

There are alternatives to clowns and magicians at children's parties as well, from people who do balloon art to theatrical plays featuring your child's favorite character. There are jugglers (and those who will teach your kid to juggle and give out balls with the goodie bags), puppet shows, artists, etc.

Entertainment at children's parties should not run more than $100, unless the supplies for what they are teaching are very expensive. Very few of us make $100 an hour.

The best place to look for children's entertainment is the local newspaper or through word of mouth from other parents. The local community center might have a bulletin board where people who want this kind of work put up fliers or business cards. You could look for ads in the yellow pages under "entertainment."

You might be able to keep the cost of children's party entertainment down by hiring students such as beauty school students, art or music students, etc. If you know someone who has a talent or hobby kids might enjoy (amateur magician, someone who could teach kids to draw comic book figures), you could ask them to share it at the party, but you have to expect to pay at least $25, and more likely $50, for their time.

Birthday parties for children and teens are really important to your child's memories of self and family, as well as those of his peers. There are certain parties and gatherings I remember from my youth that inspired me to go the extra mile for my own child. I truly believe that all it really takes is the desire to do something really special that you know your child will appreciate and the time to be as creative as you possibly can be.

A Sample Frugal Kid's At-Home Party

Amy Dacyczyn of *Tightwad Gazette* fame writes that she can throw a child's party for $25. Since she doesn't state how many kids are invited, I'll assume it's about ten kids. This is only possible if you make all your own decorations and party favors, or you have a lot of the things you will need on hand.

I think you have to have some store-bought items, especially for younger kids, so my bare-bones party comes in at about $35 (all party items are purchased at the dollar store or a party store). You can do it for about $25 if you use plain white plates and tablecloth and make your own hats and party bags.

Party for 10

Party hats	$ 1
Tablecloth	$ 1
Plates	$ 1
Cups	$ 1
Hot dogs	$ 2
Buns	$ .99
Home made sheet cake	$ 2
Candles	$ 1
Ice cream (half-gallon of store brand)	$ 2
Soda (two 2-liter bottles)	$ 2

Goodie bag contents	$10
(box of four crayons, erasers, stickers, maze puzzle, three mini-peanut butter cups, two pieces of bubble gum, fruit roll-up, Toosie pop)	
1 bag of mini–peanut butter cups	$ 1.99
1 bag of bubble gum	$ 1
16 Tootsie pops	$ 1
box of fruit roll-ups	$ 2
Prizes for games and piñata	$ 4
Bag of balloons	$ 1
Total	**$34.98**

The extra candy and treats listed above should be used as piñata stuffing.

You can spend less on prizes and games if you luck into good prizes at great prices, like a four-pack of Spiderman comics for $1.

You can just about double the price of the party for ten more kids. If you have pizza delivered instead of hot dogs, that will double the cost of the food (although you could make homemade pizza for the same price as the hot dogs).

As I mentioned, I usually budget about $100 for my son's parties. The additional $30 I would spend for a kids' party for twenty would be for the extras like mozzarella sticks and marinara sauce, extra goodies in the bags, art and crafts. If my son has a specific theme for the party and I can't make my own stuff (or if I did find the perfect store-bought party favors), some of this extra money goes into paper goods as well.

I find I am often expected to have food for the parents of the kids who come to the party (especially if it's family who has traveled a bit), so I would have to order an extra pizza or two for the adults (or order a giant sub sandwich for them), make at least one pot of coffee, and serve them cake (so the sheet cake has to feed forty or I have to make two cakes).

11

Hiring Help, Halls, and Entertainment

Having the right help, renting the right place, and hiring the right entertainment are essential, though we often take these things for granted until we have to do them ourselves.

Having the right help often makes the difference between a really great, fun party and one where the hosts are so harried you wonder why they even bothered to have a party in the first place. Good music and entertainment can make the difference between a good party and a great party.

Where you hold the party, how good the acoustics are, and whether or not there's enough space to dance and mingle is also important. How many times have you gone to a party only to leave as soon as possible because there was no room to move?

There's really only one way to be sure about the quality of the help, entertainment, and facilities, and that's to ask around and get referrals. Get on the phone to other people you know who have had the kind of party you're throwing and ask if they liked the musicians they hired or the caterer. Put together a simple list of questions that are important to you ("Was the food fresh?" "Did the musicians take longer breaks than you expected?" "Did the clown seem to like kids?"). You'd be surprised how asking the right question can bring out information that can help you make up your mind about something.

My office-mates and I recently had an office party for 120 people, and we decided to have it catered with cold cuts and dips. We called a number of people whom we knew threw regular office parties to ask about caterers, and were surprised that some of the companies that were highly recommended were actually overpriced and not as good as they seemed (they just had a lot of corporate accounts). It made it easy for us to go with a local caterer whose prices were substantially lower.

Hiring Help

We also thought about hiring a bartender or someone to pour drinks, but then decided it would be much too complicated (and costly) to set up a bar in our office. We simply set up a table with opened bottles of wine, water and soda and let people pour their own drinks and throw away their own glasses, which worked out fine. Sometimes, when you reevaluate things you find you don't need all the help you thought you would. It's definitely best to discover this before the party.

Most people need a hand in setting up and serving for a large group. While you can hire people through a professional agency (and this is important if you have unsecured valuables in your home, because many of these agencies are bonded), the cost of the help is quite steep and usually comes with hourly minimums. You can find listings for agencies that hire out bartenders, cooks, waiters, and waitresses in the yellow pages or advertised in local newspapers under temp agencies. Look for an agency that specializes in food service. If you're using a caterer, they often supply the help for serving.

If you know someone who works in a restaurant, ask if they have any friends or acquaintances who might be interested in making extra money helping out at a party. Also try calling the employment center of a local college.

Once you've found some people to help you out, ask them to dress in a white shirt and dark pants or skirt, and you should be set. As long as you don't require someone with specific skills (such as a real bartender or chef), you should be able to find people to help you out in a party.

I'm a true believer in hiring teenagers. There are so few regular jobs for kids and working part-time is a great way to learn about life. I get my teenage help through word of mouth (I asked around in my building if there were any teenagers interested in part-time work), at the local community center, and through local churches. These are great reference sources.

For help in setting up, serving, and cleaning up, I pay between $5 and $10 an hour, depending on age, difficulty of the job, and experience. Twenty dollars for an extra pair of hands at an important function or a wild children's party is nothing compared to the stress of having to do everything myself.

I always offer to feed those who have helped me, and give them leftovers to take home as well. I also give them a $10 tip each.

Hiring Entertainment

If a party requires entertainment, then the entertainment better be good. I'm amazed at how many big parties I go to where the music is lousy (or the musicians seem to have more breaks than time playing) or the performers seem to be listless and uninterested in keeping us entertained.

I once went to a children's party where the magician scared half the kids. His repertoire of tricks was just too mature for these kids (three-year-olds) and he never bothered to make his act more kid-friendly. When I carefully asked the parents how they had found him, they told me they had seen an ad in a local newspaper and had never bothered to see his performance before they hired him.

My rule of thumb in this area is to always see the entertainment you're hiring in person. A tape of the musicians is okay, but you should still see if you can drop by when they're playing at a function, just to see what they sound like on the job.

Don't allow yourself to be bullied by the entertainment into paying what you cannot afford. You've got to know the going rate for entertainment (as well as catering) or you will get taken advantage of. Ask friends or colleagues for their experience with these things. Make a few calls from newspapers and phone books so you can get an idea of what things run. I usually tell them over the phone that I'm just beginning my search and that I'm looking for pricing information. I ask them to fax me some information and a price sheet. Those that don't have something to fax or send me, and try to give me the big schmooze over the phone ("I don't have a video tape of my act—you've just got to come see me this weekend") already tells me that they're less professional.

This also goes for videographers and photographers. I need to see a price sheet, and I need to see a sample video of an affair like the one I am asking them to tape (a bar mitzvah, dinner honoring someone, awards ceremony, etc.). If I don't feel like I'm getting a professional for a fair price, I'd rather give an amateur a shot at it for a discounted price, and I make that very clear when I go into negotiations. I like to have references for things like this, but that's not always possible (and often useless, because the person you call could be a relative).

Once I've seen or heard a performer's work, I do try to see a live performance. It's a double bonus if you can see the performance in the same location that you'll be having your party, but that's only likely to happen if you got the referral from the hall where your party is being held.

Many performers, and some service providers, want you to sign a contract before the event, where they spell out how many hours they will work, how additional hours can be negotiated, etc. This is where you should be able to catch any additional charges that were not discussed, like transportation charges or travel fees. I think the signing of this kind of contract is fine if you agree to the terms. Do not rush into signing something. Ask to take it home and fax or mail the signed copy back. Ask questions about anything that doesn't seem clear to you.

Some performers want a down payment before the day of the event. This can be as little as 10 percent and as much as 50 percent. I'm not crazy about this, but I do understand that there can be travel and setup out-of-pocket costs, so something along a 10 to 25 percent deposit fee is probably fair. More than that should make you suspicious. You should pay everything by check, especially if this is office or organization related. This way you have a written record of all expenses. I would not pay performers with cash or personal credit cards.

Of course, you have to tip the performers after the party. Ten percent is customary. If you think they did a great job, you might want to give a little more. If they did an absolutely terrible job (they were late, unprepared, didn't have the right music, you paid for four musicians and only got three, etc.) you can skip the tip. If they ask why, let them know. Tips are usually in cash.

Don't be afraid to be creative in hiring entertainment. You can always contact music schools (in New York, we have Juilliard and the High School of Performing Arts). Young, wannabe professionals are often eager to begin entertaining.

Another thing you could do is rent gaming equipment, such as a roulette table, instead of music. You have to check the local laws in your area, but these kinds of parties are always enjoyed by those who attend. Gaming equipment listings can be found in the yellow pages under Entertainment. If the hall has a stage, or something like a stage, you could also hire a comedian or a hypnotist to entertain or have some kind of show, such as dancers.

Renting a Hall or Party Space

You usually rent a hall or community room for large parties of 100 people or more. These events are for things like weddings, bar and bat mitzvahs, anniversary parties, receptions, awards and retirement dinners, fund-raisers, etc.

You can find listings for halls and party space in the yellow pages under Reception Halls, Ballrooms, Caterers, or Rental Space. The local newspaper might also have listings or ads featuring community space that is available for parties.

However, one of the best ways to find space for your party is either by asking the host of a party you enjoyed for a reference, or using your connections to rent space that is not available to everyone (university club memberships, church and synagogue space, professional clubs, etc.) because these will usually be nicer and less expensive.

When I was engaged, I was the publisher of a small community newspaper and so I was invited to a lot of political fund-raising events. One of these events was in a Manhattan hotel and I quite liked the food and the decor. When my parents and I were looking for a hotel to have my wedding reception in, I remembered this fund-raiser and used the politician's name as a reference for the banquet manager. The first price he quoted us was way too high, which we let him know immediately. He then asked how much we were willing to spend per person, and we were able to come up with a fantastic formal New York wedding at a suburban reception price. I am still amazed at our success to this day.

So, one of the things you should do, even if you are arranging a fund-raiser for an organization that has a good budget, is set a price in your head and try to keep to it. Don't be embarrassed to say that you budgeted the hall at a certain price and really don't have a lot of flexibility. You would be surprised at how negotiable things can be, even at the swankiest locations.

Another thing you can do is rent a tent or two for outdoor receptions or parties, if you (or the church, school, organization, etc.) have the backyard space, or you need more space for the event than you have indoors. These can be lovely events in the summer months, and the tent insures that your event can go on, rain or shine. You can find listings for places that rent tents and tables under Party Rentals and Catering in the yellow pages. Some places even rent dance floors if you want to have entertainment.

Good entertaining is all a matter of organization and creativity, as well as your personal flair. No party should ever be just like someone else's. With this book, you should be able to find your own style, at your own price.

12

Cheapskate Recipes

These are the recipes for the food described in the various chapters of this book. I chose these recipes because their ingredients can be found in any supermarket or wholesale club from Maine to Montana throughout the year, and because they are made from relatively inexpensive items. Many of them are rather simple, in taste, preparation, and ingredients. You can always dress up these recipes by adding expensive touches, such as caviar or shrimp instead of, or in addition to, chicken.

Most of these recipes are for servings of four to six. Just multiply the ingredient amounts for the number of servings you'll need.

Cheapskate Appetizers

Guacamole

1 garlic clove
1 teaspoon salt
1 very ripe Haas avocado (you can make a dent when you give it
    a gentle squeeze)
1 tablespoon fresh lemon juice
1 tablespoon chili powder

Chop the garlic into pieces and rub the mixing bowl with the garlic. Shake in the salt. Split the avocado in half and scoop the meat out of the skins and mash with a fork. Add lemon juice and chili powder and mix.

Serve with tortilla chips.

Serves 6

Hummus

1 medium garlic clove
$^1/_2$ cup sesami tahini
3 tablespoons water
Juice of 2 lemons

16-ounce can chick peas,
   mashed
$^1/_2$ teaspoon salt
Paprika for garnish

You can use a mini-food processor that holds about four cups to make this.

Put the garlic clove in the processor and chop it. Add the well-mixed tahini sauce (you will probably have to mix this together a bit in the can or in the measuring cup, because it tends to separate into the nut and the oil). Add the water and mix in the processor. It will become a paste. Add the lemon juice (I do this through the hole in the top) until the mixture becomes creamy. Water thickens the mixture, lemon juice thins it.

Wash and drain the chick peas. Add them a handful at a time to the mixture in the processor, until the whole can has been added. Add the salt. Before serving, sprinkle with paprika.

Serve with pita bread (cut into quarters) and slices of purple onion.

Serves 6

Blue Cheese Onion Dip

1 envelope onion soup mix (generic)
1 pint sour cream
$^1/_4$ cup chunky blue cheese

Mix ingredients well and serve with mini-pretzels and potato chips.

Stuffed Mushrooms

1 package fresh mushrooms
    (between 12 and 15)
$^1/_4$ cup breadcrumbs

$^1/_4$ cup Parmesan cheese
4 tablespoons olive oil
Butter (optional)

Wash mushrooms and gently remove the stems from the caps. Boil the caps and the stems for about 15 minutes or until the mushrooms turn brownish gray. Let them cool a few minutes.

Chop up the stems. Put them in a bowl with breadcrumbs and cheese. Drizzle in the olive oil. Pack the mixture generously into the mushroom caps.

Place the stuffed mushroom caps on a cookie sheet, put a spot of butter on each one, and warm in the oven or microwave as soon as the guests arrive.

Serves 6

Deviled Eggs

1 dozen large hard-boiled eggs
6 tablespoons mayonnaise
1 teaspoon dry mustard

Pinch of salt
Paprika

Shell the eggs and cut in half lengthwise. Carefully remove the yolks.

In a medium bowl, mix the yolks with mayonnaise, dry mustard, and a pinch of salt. Restuff the eggs. Garnish with paprika.

You can dress this up by sprinkling with caviar or smoked bacon bits.

Makes 24

Stuffed Tomatoes

With Tuna

1 basket cherry tomatoes
1 6-ounce can tuna (your choice of packed in water or oil)
3 tablespoons mayonnaise

Cut the tops off of the cherry tomatoes. You can save them and put them back on the stuffed tomatoes later (if you like that look) or throw them away. Gingerly remove the tomato filling from the tomato skin (a baby spoon or an espresso spoon works well).

Mix the tuna and mayonnaise into a nice creamy consistency. Gently stuff tuna into tomato shells.

WITH CREAM CHEESE AND BLUE CHEESE

1 8-ounce package whipped cream cheese
$^1/_4$ pound crumbled blue cheese

Mix well with a fork, and then stuff into cherry tomatoes

Serves 6

Homemade Salsa

4 or 5 beefsteak tomatoes, chopped	Juice of 2 lemons
6 cloves garlic, chopped	2 onions, chopped
	2 jalapeños, chopped

Mix all ingredients in a large bowl. Cover and let sit in the refrigerator for a few hours. The longer it sits, the hotter it becomes. Stir before serving.

Nachos

TACO FILLING	1 10-ounce can red beans
$^1/_2$ pound lean ground beef	1 cup salsa
1 teaspoon garlic salt	1 small jar or can sliced
1 can tomato sauce	jalapeños
1 tablespoon chili powder	2 cups shredded cheddar
1 bag tortilla chips	cheese

To make the taco meat filling, brown the ground beef in a frying pan and sprinkle with garlic salt. Drain excess fat when meat is brown. Add the tomato sauce and chili powder. Cook for 10 minutes, covered.

Line tray or plate with unbroken tortilla chips. Add a layer of taco meat or beans on the chips, add dollops of salsa and slices of jalapeno pepper and cover with shredded cheddar. Zap in the microwave for 1 minute or until cheddar cheese is melted.

To serve, put a heaping helping of sour cream and guacamole on either end of the plate for guests to dip into.

Serves 6 to 8

Cream Cheese and Salami Roll-Ups

1 8-ounce package of whipped cream cheese
$^1/_2$ pound of thinly sliced Genoa salami

Spread cream cheese in center of salami slices, leaving a little room along the edges. Roll the salami and cream cheese up and spear with a toothpick.

You can serve whole slices, half slices, or sliced slices (on their sides to look like pinwheels).

Serves 12

Cheese Ball

1 8-ounce package whipped cream cheese
$^1/_2$ pound shredded cheddar cheese
$^1/_2$ pound shredded American cheese
$^1/_2$ teaspoon lemon juice
1 tablespoon minced onion
$^1/_2$ tablespoon Worcestershire sauce
1 package of walnut pieces, chopped (you can run these through
   the food processor)

Mix all the ingredients except walnut pieces in a bowl with a fork until well blended. Roll into one large or two smaller balls. Roll into walnut pieces and refrigerate for up to an hour.

Serve with crackers.

Baked Brie With Almonds

$^1/_2$ pound wedge of Brie
$^1/_4$ pound almond slivers

Trim rind off of Brie. Place in microwave for 10 seconds. Press almond slivers into softened Brie surfaces. Place in microwave another 15 seconds.

Serve on French bread wedges or crackers.

Cheapskate Drinks

Champagne Punch

This is a family favorite.

1 10-ounce can frozen pink lemonade
2 2-liter bottles ginger ale
1 small bag frozen strawberries or fresh strawberries cut in slices
2 oranges, sliced
1 bottle inexpensive champagne
Enough ice to cover bottom of punch bowl

About a half hour before the company is set to arrive, remove the frozen lemonade from the freezer.

In a punch bowl, pour the two bottles of ginger ale over ice. Add the defrosted lemonade concentrate and stir. Add the frozen strawberries, including the liquid, and stir some more. Float the orange slices on top. Just before the guests arrive, pour in the champagne.

Serves 20

Eggnog

Homemade eggnog is delicious, but hard work. It is perfectly okay to buy one of those premade eggnog cartons on sale around the holidays and just add your own rum or bandy.

12 large eggs
1 cup sugar
1 cup bourbon

1 cup cognac
$1/2$ teaspoon salt
3 pints whipping cream

Separate the eggs, and put the whites in the refrigerator.

Using a blender, beat the yolks with the sugar until the mixture is thick and lemony-colored. Slowly add the bourbon and the cognac, blending periodically as you go. Store in the refrigerator.

About an hour and a half before your guests are due to arrive, beat the egg whites with the salt until stiff.

In a separate bowl, whip the cream. Fold the whipped cream into the chilled-yolk mixture, then fold the egg whites into that mixture. Put the whole thing back in the refrigerator for an hour.

Just before your company arrives, taste the eggnog. If it's too thick for your taste, add a cup or two of milk. Then, pour the eggnog into a punch bowl and sprinkle with nutmeg.

Serves 35

Sangria

1 4 liter jug white or red wine	$^1/_2$ cup brandy
4 liters seltzer	1 orange, cut into slices
$^1/_2$ cup sugar	1 peach, cut into slices

Mix the wine and seltzer together and pour over ice. Add the sugar and brandy, and mix. Taste to make sure it's sweet enough. Float the fruit slices on top.

Serves 35

Lemonade

1 quart water
Juice of 5 lemons
$^1/_2$ cup sugar

Mix water and lemon juice and pour over ice. Stir in sugar. Taste for sweetness.

Serves 6

Iced Tea

1 quart water
4 teabags (fruit-flavored herbal teas work well)
Sugar to taste

Heat water until boiling. Turn off heat and put the teabags in (I usually tie the bags together). Let steep 6 minutes. Add sugar. Pour into pitcher and place in refrigerator. For quicker cooling, place in metal bowl and put in freezer for 1/2 hour. (Remember to take it out!)

Serves 8

Swamp Tea

1 quart sweetened tea
1 quart pineapple juice
1 quart ginger ale

Mix and serve over ice.

Serves 12

Piña Colada

1 16-ounce can pineapple juice
2 10-ounce cans coconut milk
1 cup (dark) rum

In a blender, add ingredients to 1 tray of ice cubes. Mix until frothy. Serve in tall glassed with straws.
    Leave out rum for virgin coladas.

Serves 10

Bloody Mary

1 16-ounce can tomato juice
2 dashes Tabasco sauce, or to taste
1 tablespoon Worcestershire sauce
Juice of 1 lemon
Salt and pepper to taste
$^2/_3$ cup vodka

Mix ingredients and serve over ice in tall glasses. Add a lime wedge or a celery stalk to the glass for decorative flavoring.

Leave out vodka for Virgin Marys.

Serves 8

Frozen Margarita

3 cups margarita mix
1 cup tequila

Put the ice in a blender, add ingredients to 1 tray of ice cubes and whip until frothy. Add more ice and rewhip if it's too liquidy.

To salt glasses, moisten glass rims with lime juice and place in a dish of salt. Salt will stick to rims.

To make margaritas from scratch, you'll need:

3 cups tequila
1 cup Triple Sec
$^1/_2$ cup fresh lime juice

Pour in blender and follow the direction for a frozen margarita above.

You can always dress this up with fresh strawberries.

Serves 4

Seabreeze

3 cups cranberry juice
3 cups grapefruit juice
1 cup vodka

Mix and serve over ice. This makes a nice summer drink, and can double as a punch.

Serves 8

Egg Cream

The recipe for this is on the bottle of the U-Bet chocolate-flavor syrup, so I have to go by their measurements. Multiply for a party.

2 tablespoons chocolate syrup
6 tablespoons whole milk
$^3/_4$ cup seltzer

Use a Drinkmaster or blender to mix the ingredients, or simply pour into a tall glass and stir vigorously.

Serves 1

Cheapskate Soups

Egg and Lemon Soup

This is the Greek version of chicken soup. It's rich and light at the same time. It goes very well as a first course to leg of lamb or Greek meatballs.

1 14-ounce can chicken broth
1 cup rice or ½ cup orzo (uncooked)
3 eggs
Juice of 2 lemons

Pour chicken broth into large pot and add an equal amount of water. Cover and heat until boiling.

Cook the rice or orzo in a separate pot.

In a separate bowl, beat eggs. Slowly add the juice of the two lemons. Add the cooked rice or orzo.

When the broth has boiled for at least 15 minutes, ladle in the egg/lemon mixture, one ladleful at a time (otherwise the egg and lemon will separate). Stir after every two or three ladlefuls. Do this until the entire egg/lemon mixture has been added to the broth pot. Cover, and shake to mix well. Serve hot.

Serves 10 to 12

Gazpacho

This is a good friend's family recipe. It is a delicious soup and a great summer meal.

9 ripe medium to large
   tomatoes
1 loaf Italian bread

2 cucumbers
2 green bell peppers
2 red bell peppers

Olive oil
Red wine vinegar
1 clove garlic

1 small onion
Salt

Peel tomatoes. If they do not peel easily, poach for a few seconds, then peel.

Soak the bread in water while you cut up 8 tomatoes, 1 cucumber, 1 green and 1 red pepper. Mix the vegetables and 1/4 of the bread in a bowl. Take a portion of this and place in the blender, adding oil, vinegar, garlic, and half the onion and salt to taste (you will need to do a few batches). Strain and refrigerate.

Cut up the remaining tomato, cucumber, peppers, and onion. Cut the rest of the Italian bread into 1-inch cubes. When you serve the cold soup, put out an array of garnishes and let your guests choose what they'd like to add.

Serves 8

Galatian Broth

This is a wonderful winter soup that is really a meal in itself, especially if served with homemade bread.

3 large potatoes
6 slices bacon or ham
3 garlic cloves, chopped
1 10-ounce can chick peas

2 cups water
Juice of 1 lemon
1 teaspoon vinegar
Salt to taste

Boil the potatoes for about 20 minutes, let cool, and peel.

Slice bacon or ham into strips. In a medium saucepan, fry the bacon. When it gets crispy, add the garlic. Pour out the bacon grease, leaving about a quarter inch. (If using ham, add some butter.) Add the chick peas, and their liquid, as well as the water.

Let the mixture boil, mashing some of the chick peas and potatoes with a fork to thicken the soup. Add the lemon juice and vinegar. Stir and boil about 15 minutes. Salt to taste. Serve hot.

Serves 6

Cheapskate Roasts

Turkey

10- to 20-pound turkey
Garlic salt
Pepper
5 slices bacon

In the morning, soak the turkey in cold water, changing the water every half hour or so (about 6 to 8 hours).

About 3½ hours before your company is set to arrive, remove the neck and gizzards from the turkey cavity and discard.

Preheat oven to 350° F.

Sprinkle garlic salt and pepper on the turkey to taste. Lay the five slices of bacon over the turkey breast. They will help baste the turkey as it cooks, and the baked bacon tastes wonderful (especially crumbled up in salad).

Most supermarket turkeys have a thermometer in the breast that pops up when the bird is done. You'll need at least 2½ hours for a 10-pound turkey, and up to 4 hours for a 20-pounder.

Add a quarter-inch of water to the bottom of the roasting pan, and check every half hour to make sure it's still there (this should ensure that the turkey doesn't stick to the pan, although the bacon grease helps there too). Baste occasionally.

Serves 12 to 25

Roast Beef

10- to 12-pound roast
Garlic salt
Pepper

Look for an eye round or sirloin tip (try to find it for $1.99 per pound or less) that's not too marbled or veiny.

Defrost the meat the day of the dinner.

Preheat oven to 400° F.

Sprinkle the meat with garlic salt and pepper. Place in roasting pan with a quarter-inch of water, basting occasionally. Cook for 2¹/₂ hours for a well-done roast. For rarer tastes, check it after 2 hours.

Serves 10 to 15

Leg of Lamb

10- to 20-pound leg of lamb
4 garlic cloves, chopped
Oregano

Defrost meat the day of the party.

About 4 hours before your guests are to arrive, preheat the oven to 400° F.

Wash the lamb and coat by hand with the chopped garlic. Sprinkle generously with oregano. Add about a quarter-inch of water to the roasting pan, and cook for 3 hours, basting occasionally.

An hour before dinner, turn the oven down to 350°F. Add a little more water to the pan. To test for doneness, pierce the leg of lamb with a long fork. If blood runs from the lamb, cook longer.

Serves 12 to 22

Roast Pork

Pernil

This is my mother-in-law's recipe, and it is delicious!

10- to 12-pound loin of pork roast
3 cloves garlic
¹/₂ cup sour orange juice (Seville orange juice) or a mixture of
    lemon and orange juice
2 tablespoons oregano
water

If the roast is frozen, begin defrosting the morning of the dinner.

Three hours before the guests are to arrive, wash the meat. Put the garlic in a food processor with the sour orange juice, oregano, and water. Coat the pork with the mixture.

Preheat the oven to 400° F.

Cook the roast for 1½ hours, basting occasionally. Add water to the pan as needed to keep the roast from sticking. Test for doneness with a fork. If it's tender, it's done.

Serves 12 to 15

Gravy

2 cups water
Salt and pepper
Soy sauce
Flour

Add water to the pan drippings (2 cups to make 1 bowl of gravy, 4 cups for 2). Place the roasting pan on the stovetop so that it can be heated by two burners at the same time. Add a little salt and pepper and a dash or two of soy sauce. Add flour (I like to use Wondra Quick Mixing Flour for Gravies) a dusting at a time, while stirring the heating mixture. Add more flour to thicken, add more water to thin.

2 cups

Fancy Gravy

1 cup white or red wine
½ cup heavy cream

Add white or red wine to pan drippings. Boil the mixture down by one-third, stirring with a fork to scrape up any additional drippings. Add the cream, and heat without bringing to a boil. Strain into a gravy bowl.

Coq au Vin

Ask your butcher to cut up a whole chicken for you, or buy an assortment of legs, wings, and breasts—it may be cheaper that way.

1 whole chicken cut into serving pieces	1 clove garlic
Flour	3 slices ham, in thin strips
$^{1}/_{2}$ cup (1 stick) butter	$^{1}/_{4}$ teaspoon thyme
8 small potatoes	1 bay leaf
10 small carrots	2 ounces warmed cognac
10 small onions	1 cup dry red wine
10 small, whole mushrooms	(like a Bordeaux)

Preheat the oven to 300° F. Coat the chicken pieces with flour and fry in butter on the stove until browned. In a large, covered casserole dish, add the potatoes, carrots, onions, mushrooms, garlic, ham, thyme, and bay leaf, and then put the chicken pieces on top of that layer.

Pour the cognac over the chicken and ignite. When the alcohol has burned off, add the wine.

Cover and bake, about 2$^{1}/_{2}$ hours.

Serves 6

Cheapskate Vegetables and Sides

Mashed Potatoes

6 to 10 medium potatoes
3 tablespoons butter
3 or 4 tablespoons cream or milk

Salt
Pepper

Add potatoes to rapidly boiling water and cover for 20 minutes.

Drain and run under cold water. Remove the skins and mash the potatoes in the pot with a potato masher. Add butter (about a pat per potato) and mix until melted. Add cream or milk and stir. The more milk and cream, the creamier the potatoes. Add salt and pepper to taste. You can add a diced garlic clove or garlic salt after the potatoes are mashed, but before serving, if you want garlic mashed potatoes.

Serves 8 to 10

Stuffed Artichokes

This is a lot of work, but worth it if you really want to impress or show someone that you think they're special. In spring and fall you can get two or three artichokes for $1.

4 artichokes (or one for each guest)
2 tablespoons butter
1 cup bread crumbs
1 cup shredded cheddar cheese
$^1/_4$ cup Parmesan cheese

Boil artichokes, about 20 minutes. Drain and cool slightly. When you can hold them, gently loosen apart the outer leaves without pulling them off, until you can reach the fine leaves toward the center. Remove these, either with your fingers or with tongs that have a good grip. When you reach the center of the artichoke, scrape off the heart's hair. This gets easier with practice. You should have a nice open center in which you can place the stuffing.

To prepare the stuffing, melt the butter. Mix the remaining ingredients in a bowl, then add the melted butter and mix. When you have emptied all artichoke centers, stuff them with the filling. Push some of the outer leaves of the artichoke open and place some of the stuffing between each leaf.

Heat the stuffed artichokes for about 10 minutes or until the cheddar cheese in the stuffing is melted. Serve hot. I also serve this dish with side plates for discarded leaves.

Serves 4

Stuffed Celery

1 bunch celery
1 8-ounce package of whipped cream cheese
$^1/_2$ pound blue cheese (crumbled preferred)
Paprika

Wash celery and cut off stalks and heart. Cut stalks into six-inch-long pieces (you should have about 20 to 25).

Mix the cream cheese and blue cheese until smooth. Use a fork to stuff the celery stalks and smooth over the tops. Arrange on a tray. Sprinkle with paprika for garnish. Refrigerate until the guests arrive.

20 to 25 celery sticks

Lemon-Butter Broccoli

2 bunches broccoli
$^1/_4$ cup ($^1/_2$ stick) of butter
Juice of $^1/_2$ lemon

Wash the broccoli and cut into florets. Steam them for about 10 minutes.

Melt the butter. Mix with the lemon juice. Toss lemon-butter mixture with broccoli florets before serving.

Salad

If I've made hummus for my guests I will have reserved a handful of chick peas, which I will throw into the salad. If I've made a roast turkey, I will crumble up some of the bacon that got roasted with it and throw that in the salad.

2 heads of green or red leaf lettuce
2 or 3 plum tomatoes
1 red or yellow onion
$^1/_4$ cup olives
Croutons
Handful of walnuts or pignoli nuts
Blue cheese (optional)

Wash lettuce and tomatoes. Tear lettuce leaves into a large salad bowl. Slice tomatoes and onions. Add remaining ingredients and toss with a vinaigrette dressing.

Serves 10 to 16

Greek Salad

Salad (see preceding recipe)
$^1/_4$ pound feta cheese, crumbled
12–20 Kalamata olives
1 green pepper, sliced into rings

Make the salad as described in the preceding recipe and add crumbled pieces of feta cheese, the Kalamata olives, and green pepper slices, if you have some on hand.

Serves 10 to 16

Waldorf Salad

This salad was supposedly invented and served at the Waldorf Astoria. It's delicious, and rarely served, so people remember it.

1 head of red leaf lettuce
2 apples
2 carrots
$^1/_4$ pound shelled walnuts
Raspberry vinaigrette
2 tablespoons crumbled blue cheese

Wash and shred the lettuce. Peel and core the apples and cut into thin slices or chunks. Slice the carrots and break up the walnuts into bite-sized pieces. Douse in a raspberry vinaigrette dressing and sprinkle on the blue cheese. Toss.

Vinaigrette Dressing

1 tablespoon salt
3 tablespoons olive oil
1 tablespoon red wine or balsamic vinegar (raspberry or tarragon vinegar works too)
1 teaspoon Dijon honey mustard

Cover the bottom of the cup or glass you're mixing the vinaigrette in with a dusting of salt. Add three parts olive oil to one part vinegar, to half-part mustard. Mix with a fork or whisk.

Cornbread Stuffing

1 box Jiffy cornbread mix
1 tablespoon butter
1 chopped onion
1 diced green pepper

$^1/_2$ cup of canola oil
$^1/_2$ cup walnuts
$^1/_2$ cup raisins

Follow Jiffy cornbread mix directions for making cornbread (about 20 minutes). Let cool about five minutes.

In a large pot, melt butter and brown the onions and peppers. Cut the cornbread into half-inch cubes and mix into the butter, onions, and peppers. Add a little canola oil, and toss. Add the walnuts and raisins. Stir. Add more canola oil until the stuffing doesn't seem too dry. Cover and heat on medium heat for five minutes.

For Thanksgiving, add cranberries to the recipe.

Potato Salad

10 potatoes	3 tablespoons mayonnaise
6 eggs	1 tablespoon mustard
2 onions, chopped	Salt and pepper to taste

Boil potatoes for 20 minutes. Ten minutes into boiling, gently add the eggs to the pot.

Chop onions while waiting for potato and eggs to finish cooking.

When potatoes and eggs are done, drain and pour cold water over them. Remove the eggs and let them soak in cold water, then remove shells.

Remove yolks and mash together in a small bowl. Add mayonnaise and mustard, and sprinkle with salt and pepper to taste.

Chop up egg whites and put in a big bowl with onions.

Peel potatoes and chop into cubes or chunks. Mix with onions and egg whites. Mix in yolk dressing. If it appears that there's not enough dressing, add more mayonnaise. Serve chilled.

You can always add fresh peas and/or crumbled bacon bits.

Serves 10 to 12

Cole Slaw

2 heads of cabbage, shredded or cut into thin strips
1 large onion, shredded
1^1/$_2$ cups mayonnaise
4 tablespoons sugar
2 tablespoons lemon juice
^{1}/$_4$ teaspoon salt
^{1}/$_4$ teaspoon pepper
2 tablespoons cream or milk

Toss cabbage and onions together in a large bowl.

In a small bowl, mix mayonnaise, sugar, lemon juice, salt and pepper. Stir in cream or milk.

Pour dressing over cabbage and onion mixture and toss. Chill until ready to serve.

Serves 12 to 15

Rice and Beans

This is my mother-in-law's recipe. You can freeze any leftover beans in plastic bags.

1 16-ounce package dry red beans
1 onion, chopped
2 tablespoons garlic salt
Fresh cilantro
2 tablespoons olive oil
1 tablespoon red wine vinegar
4 cups water
2 tablespoons olive oil
2 cups white enriched rice

Soak the beans in cold water in a large pot overnight.

Drain the beans. Follow package directions for cooking, adding chopped onion, garlic salt, some sprigs of cilantro, and olive oil to the beans. Stir occasionally. Simmer for 1 hour, then add wine vinegar. Continue to simmer.

When the beans begin to thicken, stir and cook another 1/2 hour. When you can easily mash the beans, taste them and see if they're ready. Keep warm.

Prepare the rice. Bring water with olive oil to boil in medium saucepan. Add rice, return to the boil, then lower heat, cover, and let simmer for 20 minutes.

Serve beans over rice.

Serves 20

Chicken Tarragon Salad

2 cooked chicken breasts
1 small onion, quartered
2 tablespoons mayonnaise
2 teaspoons dried tarragon

Place chicken meat and onion in food processor and chop. Transfer chopped meat and onion into a bowl. Add mayonnaise and tarragon. Serve on crackers or croissants with lettuce.

Serves 4

Curried Tuna Salad

1 6-ounce can albacore tuna
2 tablespoons mayonnaise
2 teaspoons curry powder, or to taste
1 $1^{1}/_{4}$-ounce box raisins
Handful of walnuts

Mix ingredients in a bowl until well blended. Serve on pita bread cut into small wedges or as sandwiches.

Serves 6

Cheapskate Casseroles, Pasta, and Meat Dishes

Shrimp Scampi

This is the only recipe for which I ever used the electric frying pan I got as a wedding present, but it's worth keeping it just for this. But you can use a regular frying pan.

1¹/₂ cups olive oil
1 pound linguine
¹/₂ cup (1 stick) salted butter, cut into pieces
8 medium to large garlic cloves, chopped
1¹/₂ tablespoons red pepper flakes
36 peeled and deveined shrimp (about ³/₄ of a pound)
1 green bell pepper, cut into pieces
1 red bell pepper, cut into pieces
¹/₃ cup fresh lemon juice
¹/₄ cup chopped fresh parsley

Boil water for linguine. Add 1 tablespoon olive oil. Add pasta. Cook for 12 minutes, until al dente. Drain linguine and set aside.

In a large frying pan, heat the olive oil and butter over a moderate to high heat. Add the garlic and pepper flakes and saute for about 30 seconds.

Add the shrimp and peppers and saute for 2 or 3 minutes, until the shrimp turn pink. Gently stir in the lemon juice and parsley. Serve over cooked linguine with grated Parmesan cheese, if desired.

Serves 6

Pasta Carbonara

1 pound linguini or spaghetti
1 tablespoon olive oil
3 tablespoons butter
$^3/_4$ pound bacon (about 10 slices), cut into $^1/_2$ -inch slices
3 medium garlic cloves
6 egg yolks
2 cups heavy cream
2 cups grated Parmesan cheese, divided

Boil water for linguine or spaghetti. Add olive oil. Cook pasta for 10 to 12 minutes, until al dente. Drain and set aside.

In a frying pan, melt the butter and fry the bacon until crisp, about 3 to 5 minutes (or microwave the bacon, then add to frying pan). Drain off most of the bacon fat. Sauté the garlic for about 1 minute in the remaining grease.

In a bowl, beat the egg yolks, cream and $1^1/_2$ cups of the Parmesan cheese.

Add cooked, drained pasta to the frying pan and pour in the cream mixture. Toss over a low heat until the sauce thickens and coats the pasta, about 2 to 3 minutes. Serve hot with remaining Parmesan cheese.

Serves 6

Macaroni and Cheese

2 8-ounce packages of elbow macaroni
2 8-ounce packages Velveeta
6 tablespoons ($^3/_4$ stick) butter
$^1/_2$ cup flour
4 cups hot milk
$^1/_2$ teaspoon Worcestershire sauce
$^1/_4$ teaspoon red or black pepper
$^1/_3$ cup bread crumbs

Cook elbow macaroni according to instructions on the box. Drain and set aside.

Preheat oven to 375° F.

Grease a large casserole dish or two smaller dishes with 2 table-spoon of butter. Cut up Velveeta into chunks or slices.

In a large saucepan melt 3/5 of the butter. Stir in flour until smooth. Using a whisk, stir in milk all at once and continue stirring until it comes to a boil. Cook for one minute longer, then remove from heat and add Worcestershire sauce. Add Velveeta chunks and stir until melted. Stir in cooked macaroni and pepper. Pour into casserole dish.

Sprinkle bread crumbs over the top of the macaroni and cheese and bake for 30 to 35 minutes, until the casserole bubbles and browns slightly on top.

For variety, you can cut back on the Velveeta and use cheddar cheese or even something like feta, as long as the cheese is sharp.

Poor Man's Paella

The real stuff is supposed to have a lot more seafood, but that's quite expensive, so I've cut back. To impress, add lobster meat, crabmeat, or scallops.

If you can't find saffron, or you're lucky and you can find Vitarroz saffron rice for paella, buy three packages of this and use it as the rice base—just add the meat and fish and spices.

1 3-pound chicken, cut up in pieces
3 tablespoons olive oil
2 chorizos (spicy Spanish sausage), sliced into $^1/_2$-inch rounds
1 onion, chopped
2 cloves garlic, chopped
1 8-ounce can of tomato sauce
1 teaspoon oregano
1 teaspoon wine vinegar
$2^1/_2$ cups enriched rice
4 cups boiling water
1 teaspoon saffron
$^1/_2$ pound (about 15 to 20) cooked small to medium shrimp,
   peeled and deveined
1 8-ounce can of peas
1 4-ounce can of clams
15 Spanish olives, sliced

In a large frying pan, brown the chicken pieces in 1 tablespoon of the olive oil. Before they are done, add sliced chorizos, chopped onion, and garlic. Cook about 5 minutes over low heat. Add tomato sauce, oregano, vinegar, the rest of the oil, and the rice and cook for 5 minutes. Add boiling water, saffron, and peeled shrimp. Turn up heat a bit and cover. Simmer for about 20 minutes, or until the liquid is absorbed. Add peas, clams, and diced olives and stir. Cook about 5 more minutes and serve.

Serves 10

To double this recipe, I make it in a large spaghetti pot with a lid—the lid is important to ensure the rice is properly cooked.

Jambalaya

1 onion, chopped
1 green bell pepper, chopped
2 garlic cloves, chopped
2 tablespoons butter
1 cup pieces of cooked chicken meat
$^1/_2$ pound of cooked ham, cut in cubes or slices
2 chorizos, sliced into $^1/_2$ -inch rounds
1 12-ounce can tomatoes
1 cup enriched rice
$1^1/_2$ cups chicken broth
$^1/_2$ teaspoon thyme
1 tablespoon chopped fresh parsley or flakes
$^1/_2$ teaspoon chili powder
Pinch of salt and pepper

Preheat over to 350° F.

Sauté the onions, green pepper, and garlic in the butter, until tender. Add chicken, ham, and chorizos and cook for about 5 minutes. Add tomatoes with their liquid, rice, broth, and spices. Stir and cook for 5 minutes.

Transfer to a covered casserole dish and bake for $1^1/_2$ hours.

If you want to make this ahead of time, to serve later, bake for an hour and refrigerate. When ready to serve, put it in the oven for 1/2 hour to warm.

Serves 6

Ham, Cheese, and Spaghetti Casserole

1 pound spaghetti
1 package Velveeta cheese
1 small smoked ham, enough for 3 cups, cubed
2 tablespoons ($^1/_4$ stick) butter
1 cup milk
$^1/_4$ cup flour
2 tablespoons mustard
1 small can tomato sauce
8 slices mozzarella

Cook and drain spaghetti, and set aside.

Preheat oven to 350° F.

Cut Velveeta into cubes.

In a saucepan, melt the butter, add flour, and whisk together. Heat the milk in a separate pan and add to the flour and butter mixture. Add the Velveeta and stir until creamy. Add the mustard and ham.

Put spaghetti in casserole dish and pour in cheese mixture. Pour the tomato sauce over the top of the casserole and arrange mozzarella slices on top.

Bake for 30 to 35 minutes, until casserole bubbles and the mozzarella slices are browned.

Serve with garlic bread.

Serves 10

Meatloaf

Meatloaf is a favorite food for most guys, so it's great for a guy party, such as a Super Bowl, poker game, or a bachelor party.

$1^1/_2$ pounds ground beef	$^1/_2$ tablespoon oregano
1 cup seasoned bread crumbs	1 tablespoon
1 onion, chopped	Worcestershire sauce
1 egg	$^1/_2$ teaspoon dry mustard
1 cup milk	$^1/_4$ teaspoon sage
1 tablespoon garlic salt	1 clove garlic, chopped

Preheat oven to 350° F.

In a large bowl, mix all ingredients until well combined. (I do it by hand, rings removed). Put the meat mixture in a bread pan and pat down.

Bake uncovered for 1½ hours.

Serve with mashed potatoes and gravy.

For quick beef gravy: Boil 1/2 cup water and add beef bouillon and 1 tablespoon of butter. When bouillon is melted, add a dash of soy sauce and stir in Wondra flour until thick.

Serves 6

Lasagna

1 pound ground beef
1 medium onion, chopped
2 cloves garlic, pressed
1 16-ounce can whole tomatoes
1 15-ounce can tomato sauce
3 tablespoons fresh chopped parsley or flakes
Leaf or two of fresh basil
Pinch of salt
16-ounces ricotta cheese
½ cup grated Parmesan cheese
1 tablespoon oregano
½ pound (about 9 or 10) cooked lasagna noodles
2 cups (8 ounces) mozzarella cheese, shredded or sliced

Brown the ground beef, onions, and garlic and drain excess fat. Add canned tomatoes with liquid, tomato sauce, 2 tablespoons of the parsley, basil, and salt. Heat to boiling, stirring occasionally. Simmer one hour uncovered, until thick. Set aside.

Mix ricotta cheese, 1/4 cup of the Parmesan cheese, rest of parsley, a pinch of salt, and oregano.

In an oblong baking pan, make three layers noodles, tomato-meat sauce, and cheese mixture. Pour remaining sauce over the top. Sprinkle top with reserved 1/4 cup Parmesan and shredded mozzarella.

Bake uncovered for 45 minutes. Let sit for 10 minutes before serving.

Serve with garlic bread and salad.

Serves 10

For a vegetable lasagna, don't use meat in the sauce. Add vegetables, like chopped spinach or sliced zucchini. Add two beaten eggs to the cheese filling and follow the same directions as above.

Some people make a vegetable lasagna without the noodles, substituting sliced zucchini or eggplant that has been dipped in flour, eggs, and bread crumbs.

Pastichio

GREEK LASAGNA

You can leave the meat out of recipe if your guests are vegetarians or if you are having another meat course.

1 onion, chopped
$^1/_2$ pound (2 sticks) butter, plus 2 tablespoons
2 pounds lean ground lamb or beef
$^1/_2$ teaspoon cinnamon
Sprinkle nutmeg or allspice
$^1/_2$ cup water
$^1/_2$ cup dry red wine
1 pound ziti
1 cup grated Parmesan cheese
1 pound box filo pastry
6 large eggs
5 cups milk
$^1/_4$ cup bread crumbs

Preheat oven to 350° F.

Sauté onion in 2 tablespoons butter until golden. Add the meat and cook slowly until brown. Add spices, water, and wine. Simmer for 5 minutes and remove from the heat.

Cook ziti in salted water and drain; return ziti to pot. Add remaining butter to ziti and stir, until butter melts and the pasta is well covered. Add 3/4 cup of the grated Parmesan cheese and mix well. Melt some of the butter and set aside.

Butter an 11 × 15 × 2 pan and layer with filo sheets, buttering each sheet, extending the sheets past the ends of the pan (the overhanging pastry will be used to enclose the mixture later on).

Spoon half the ziti over the filo sheets and spread evenly. Pour all the meat mixture over the ziti, and spread the remaining ziti on top.

Beat the eggs very well. Add the milk and continue beating a few minutes. Pour this mixture over the meat and ziti and sprinkle with the remaining 1/4 cup of Parmesan. Fold up the overhanging filo ends to cover sides. Cover the entire top with another 6 or 8 buttered filo sheets and bake for about 1 hour.

Serves 20

Greek Meatballs

3 pounds ground lamb
Oregano or mint
3 large eggs
1$^1/_2$ cups bread crumbs

1 onion, chopped
Handful of pignoli nuts
 (optional)

Mix all the ingredients in a large bowl until well mixed. Roll the mixture into one-inch-diameter balls.

Heat an ungreased frying pan. Put in meatballs without crowding pan (about 25 at a time) and begin cooking. After about a minute, turn the meatballs. Then cover the frying pan, lower heat, and cook for about 10 minutes until done.

Serve meatballs with lemon slices, hot or cold.

Should yield about 50

Chili

This is my husband's recipe.

12 dried chipotle chiles
$^1/_2$ cup (1 stick) butter
6 pounds stew beef, cut into
 1-inch cubes
4 onions, chopped
8 garlic cloves, chopped
3 tablespoons ground cumin
1 tablespoon chili powder

2 pounds tomatoes, peeled,
 seeded, and chopped
2 bay leaves
1 teaspoon oregano
1 shot tequila
1 bottle Dos Equis dark
 beer
Salt

Heat a skillet over medium-high heat. Toast the chiles, turning frequently, for 1 to 2 minutes. Let them cool, then remove the seeds.

Combine seeded chiles with one cup water in the saucepan. Cover, bring to a boil and simmer for 5 minutes.

Transfer chili mixture to a food processor and purée.

Heat the butter in a large pot and sauté the beef, a handful at a time, until nicely browned on all sides. Transfer the meat to a heated platter.

To the hot butter and beef drippings, add the onion and garlic, and cook over medium heat, stirring until the onions are soft. Be careful not to burn the garlic. Add the cumin and chili powder, and cook, stirring, over medium-low heat for 1 minute.

Add the beef, puréed chiles, tomatoes, bay leaves, and oregano. Stir well. Add half of the beer and then just enough water to barely cover. Bring to a boil.

Take a shot of tequila while you wait for the chiles to boil. Chase with the remaining beer.

Once the chili is boiling, cover and simmer, stirring occasionally, for 2 hours. Keep adding water as necessary to keep the meat covered while cooking.

Add salt to taste. Adjust seasonings, if necessary, and simmer, uncovered, for 1 hour more. Discard bay leaves before serving.

Serves 12

Serve with the usual accompaniments: sour cream, shredded cheddar cheese, chopped onion, and cornbread. You can also serve this over rice.

Chicarones de Pollo

This is a favorite recipe of the men in my family, and one that was passed on from my mother-in-law. I have never met a man who didn't love this, and lick his fingers while eating it.

3 to 5 whole chickens, cut up in small pieces
1 20 ounce bottle lemon juice
1 6 ounce jar of garlic powder
1 cup flour for dredging
32 ounces oil for frying

The day before the party, put the chicken pieces in a roasting pan (the biggest you have) and let them soak overnight in a mixture of lemon juice and garlic powder. Put the tray in your refrigerator and turn the chicken pieces every once in a while.

The next day, when you are ready to fry, drain the chicken pieces and dry each one with a clean rag or kitchen towel. On a separate plate, roll each piece of chicken in flour.

Heat the oil until it starts to bubble. I usually use two frying pans and my electric frying pan, so that I can cook all of the chicken quickly: you don't want to crowd the pan (it cools the oil and the chicken will cook more slowly and absorb more oil). Cook the chicken pieces in the oil, turning them occasionally, until golden brown, about 10 minutes.

Place the cooked chicken on a big platter lined with paper towels to soak up oil. When all the chicken pieces are done, pat them down with paper towels. Serve hot.

Serves 30 to 40

Grilled Tuna Over Linguine

4 tablespoons olive oil
2 pounds linguine
2 (about 1 pound total) tuna steaks
2 large garlic cloves, chopped
Oregano
2 tablespoons butter

Boil 4 quarts of water. Add 1 tablespoon of olive oil to the water and cook linguine. Drain and set aside.

Rub tuna steaks with 1 chopped clove of garlic and season with oregano. Grill for 6 minutes on each side, depending upon how well-done you like your tuna. Heat remaining oil and butter with garlic until brown. Remove garlic and toss over linguine and tuna. Serve tuna pieces on top of the linguine.

Cheapskate Desserts

Pies

I use a frozen premade pie crust (about $2), but it's much cheaper to make your own. Many women make up a huge batch of pie crusts at the beginning of the summer and freeze them in plastic bags.

HOMEMADE CRUST

1 cup flour
1 teaspoon salt
²/₃ cup shortening or softened butter
¹/₃ cup cold water

Mix flour and salt. Cut shortening or butter into flour mix as best you can. Add water at little at a time, until you have a ball of dough you can roll with your hand.

Break in two and roll out with a floured roller.

APPLE FILLING

6 or 7 apples
¹/₂ cup sugar
¹/₂ cup flour
1 teaspoon each cinnamon and nutmeg

Preheat oven to 375° F.

Line the pie plate with the rolled-out crust dough.

Peel and core the apples and cut them into chunks or slices. Mix the sugar, flour, and spices together and add to apples in a large bowl. Mix until apple pieces are well-covered. Put apples into pie plate.

Cover the pie with the second piece of pie crust, folding the edges of the two crusts together. Cut excess pie crust off with a sharp knife.

Make a small hole in the center of the pie and cut four slashes into the pie, one in each quarter to let hot air escape as the pie bakes.

Cover the pie edges with thin pieces of aluminum foil. Bake for 35 minutes. Remove foil and bake another 10 minutes. Cool for at least a 1/2 hour before eating.

Serves 8 to 10.

To make a berry filling: combine 2 pints of berries with 1/2 cup sugar and 1/2 cup flour. Follow the same directions as for apple pie.

For a blueberry and raspberry pie, use 1 pint of each. For strawberry pie, use 2 pints of strawberries.

PUMPKIN

1 egg	$3/4$ teaspoon cinnamon
1 can pumpkin pie filling	$1/4$ teaspoon ground cloves
$2/3$ cup sugar	$1^1/4$ cups evaporated milk

Beat the egg, then mix with the pumpkin filling and milk. Add spices and mix until smooth. Pour into pie shell. Bake about 40 minutes. Cool. Serve with sweetened whipped cream, if desired.

Serves 8 to 10

BANANA CREAM

2 packages instant vanilla pudding
1 graham cracker crust, store-bought
1 banana, sliced
1 pint cream
2 tablespoons sugar

Follow directions on pudding package to make vanilla pudding, using slightly less milk so that the pudding is really creamy. Let cool slightly. Pour into graham cracker crust and arrange banana slices on top. Let settle in refrigerator. Meanwhile, add sugar to cream and beat with an electric mixer until stiff. Serve the pie with sweetened whipped cream.

Serves 10

For a chocolate cream pie: follow directions for banana cream pie above, substituting chocolate pudding for vanilla and leaving out the bananas.

Brownies

I use a 99-cent mix. To dress up the mix, add walnuts to the batter, and garnish cooked brownies by placing a walnut half in the center of each brownie piece (put them on while the brownies are hot). If you really want to jazz the brownies up, add Reese's Pieces to the mix.

Serve with ice cream and whipped cream, for a really wonderful dessert.

Serves 16

Oatmeal Cookies

This recipe is from the Quaker Oats box top. I just added the nuts and raisins.

1 cup (2 sticks) softened margarine or butter
$1^1/_4$ cups firmly packed brown sugar
$^1/_2$ cup sugar
2 eggs
2 tablespoons milk
2 teaspoons vanilla extract
$1^3/_4$ cups flour
1 teaspoon backing soda
$2^1/_2$ cups oats (instant or old-fashioned), uncooked
1 cup chocolate chips
$^1/_2$ cup walnuts
$^1/_2$ cup raisins

Heat oven to 375° F.

Beat softened butter and the sugars together with an electric mixer until creamy. Add eggs, milk, and vanilla and beat well. Add flour and baking soda, and mix with a spoon. Stir in oats, one cup at a time. Add chocolate chips, walnuts, and raisins and make sure they are distributed evenly throughout the thick mix.

Drop rounded tablespoons of cookie mix onto cookie sheets (about 16 per sheet). Bake for 9 or 10 minutes. Let cool a few minutes before removing from cookie sheet.

Makes about 3 dozen

Sugar Cookies

Sugar cookies are delicious and great for kids' parties because you can make them into different shapes with cookie cutters, and they taste wonderful. You have to chill the dough for a few hours, so it's best to make it the day before you make the cookies.

1 cup sugar	1 teaspoon vanilla extract
1 stick softened butter	2^1/$_2$ cups flour
2 eggs	2 teaspoons baking powder
1 to 2 tablespoons milk	

Mix sugar and butter in large bowl with an electric mixer until fluffy. Beat in eggs, milk, and vanilla.

In a separate bowl, mix flour and baking powder. Slowly add the flour mixture to the sugar and butter mixture, until it takes on a dough-like consistency. Add a bit more milk if the mixture seems very dry. Break into four equal pieces, wrap in plastic wrap and refrigerate for a few hours. (You can freeze the dough if you're not going to be making all the cookies.)

Preheat oven to 350° F

Using a floured rolling pin, roll out the chilled dough on a floured surface. If you're using cookie cutters, flour them too. Cut out cookies and transfer to the cookie sheet. Reuse scraps. Decorate to your heart's content.

Bake for 10 to 12 minutes, until slightly brown. Cool for 3 minutes before removing from sheet.

Makes 4 dozen

Rice Pudding

²/₃ cup rice	¹/₂ cup sugar
2 quarts milk, plus	1 tablespoon butter
2 tablespoons	2 teaspoons vanilla extract
Pinch of salt	Cinnamon
4 eggs	

Cook rice in the 2 quarts milk with salt added, until rice is tender (about 10 minutes), stirring frequently.

In a bowl, beat the eggs with 2 tablespoons milk and beat in the sugar.

When the rice is tender, remove from heat and add the butter. Once butter has melted, stir in the egg mixture. Place back on the heat. Bring to a gentle boil; remove from heat and add vanilla.

Spoon into a casserole dish or individual glasses. Sprinkle with cinnamon. Chill or serve slightly warm.

Serves 6 to 8

Ice Cream Cake

- 6 graham crackers
- 6 macaroons (or use more graham crackers)
- 4 tablespoons dark rum
- 4 tablespoons Kahlua
- 1 quart coffee ice cream, softened
- 2 milk chocolate bars
- 1 pint sweetened whipped cream
- Sliced almonds

In a deep glass bowl, mash the graham crackers and macaroons up, so that they line the bottom, Pour on the rum and Kahlua. Spoon the coffee ice cream on top of this, so that it forms a layer at least an inch thick (thicker if you really like coffee ice cream). Chop up the chocolate bars in the food processor, and sprinkle the pieces over the ice cream. Add a layer of whipped cream and sprinkle the almond slivers over the cream. Freeze for at least one hour before serving.

Serves 8 to 10

Trifle

To me, Trifle is kitchen sink cake, although I'm sure it once had a very rigid recipe. It's what I make over the holidays, when I have a lot of left-over dessert bits. I believe you can be as creative as you want with the recipe. The amounts used here are approximate because you often make this from leftovers.

1 box vanilla or chocolate pudding mix
1 cup chocolate, peanut butter, or white chocolate chips
$^1/_2$ pound cake or 2 slices chocolate cake, cut in cubes
4 Graham crackers, crumbed
$^1/_2$ cup chocolate or coffee liquer
Frozen strawberries or other berries
$^1/_2$ cup whipped cream
$^1/_2$ cup chocolate sauce

Prepare pudding according to instructions, stir in some chocolate pieces until melted.

In a punch bowl, cut up cake in cubes and mix with graham cracker crumbs. Drizzle with liqueur. Use half the cake for the first layer of trifle, then add half the pudding, then half the berries. Repeat. Top with whipped cream. Decorate top of trifle with leftover berries and chocolate sauce.

Serves 10 to 12

Chocolate Mousse

1 6-ounce package semisweet chocolate morsels
2 tablespoons instant coffee
$^1/_2$ cup sugar
$^1/_2$ tablespoon vanilla extract
3 eggs, separated
Whipped cream

In medium pan, combine chocolate pieces, instant coffee, 1/4 cup of the sugar, and 2 tablespoons water. Stir constantly over low flame, until chocolate is melted and sugar is dissolved. Remove from heat. With wooden spoon, beat until smooth; let cool slightly. Add vanilla. Beat in egg yolks, one at a time, beating well after each.

In a separate bowl, beat egg whites just until soft peaks form when mixer is raised. Add remaining sugar, 1 tablespoon at a time, beating well. With spatula, fold chocolate mixture into egg whites mixture until well combined. Spoon into goblets or fluted glasses. Cool 1 hour. Serve with whipped cream.

Serves 6

Cheapskate Condiments

Pesto

3 large garlic cloves	$^1/_4$ teaspoon parsley
3 cups washed basil leaves	(fresh or flakes)
$^1/_4$ cup pignoli nuts	2 tablespoons melted butter
$^1/_2$ cup Parmesan cheese	4 tablespoons olive oil

Using a mini food processor, chop the garlic cloves. Add the basil (well-packed), pignoli nuts, Parmesan cheese, and parsley. Chop a little, then add the melted butter through hole in center of processor. Add half the olive oil. When the consistency turns creamy, taste. Add olive oil if you feel it needs more body. Toss over any kind of cooked pasta.

If you leave out the butter and cheese, this freezes well and lasts months. Add cheese and butter before using.

Herbed and Flavored Butters

For herbed butter for meat, add 1 tablespoon of tarragon or chopped garlic to 1/4 pound (1 stick) softened butter.

For a fruited butter for breakfast breads, add mashed strawberries to 1/4 pound (1 stick) of softened butter. Or for another breakfast butter, add 1 tablespoon of honey.

Chill the flavored butter in a small dish or a mold, then serve.

Fancy Cream Cheese

Mix 1 8-ounce package of whipped cream cheese with with chopped scallions or chopped Spanish olives. Chill before serving.

Barbecue Sauce

$^1/_3$ cup Dijon mustard
$^1/_3$ cup molasses
$^1/_3$ cup apple cider vinegar

Mix and brush over meat.

Enough for large ribs or chicken for 6

Steak Marinade

1 onion, chopped
2 cloves garlic, chopped
1 teaspoon fresh chopped or dried parsley
Juice of 1 lemon
Salt

Mix all ingredients and marinate steaks for one hour prior to cooking.

Covers 3 or 4 individual steaks

Resources

This list is by no means comprehensive. It is just a compilation of the resources and references that I use when I'm planning a party.

I'm sure that readers will have their own sources. I would love to hear from you, if you have suggestions to add to my list. E-mail me at Lori_Perkins@yahoo.com or write to me at Perkins, Rubie & Associates, 240 W. 35 St., No. 500, New York, N.Y. 10001.

Web Sites and Newsgroups

Most of the women's magazines have web sites with forums where readers can read up on any topic from recipes to beauty. My favorite is *Redbook*'s Home Arts Web site at www.homearts.com They have a party planner forum, where you can read discussions on all sorts of parties, as well as leave messages for other readers to get back to you with their ideas and experiences. They also have a number of forums with recipes and an in-house chef who will E-mail you ideas. There's even a frugality forum.

Some other recipe sites are:

www.kitchenlink.com
www.culinary.com
www.epicurious.com (*Gourmet* magazine online)
www.compucook.com

Remember, that many of these recipe sites are not concerned about the cost of the meals they suggest, so you have to be the judge of how expensive they will be for your party.

A frugality newsgroup I belong to is morewithless@geocities.com This is a forum for people who are trying to keep an eye on costs in all areas of their lives.

For children's party ideas that include arts and crafts as well as an occasional menu, I would recommend:

www.seussville.com
www.nick.com
www.disney.com
www.kidswarnerbros.com
www.dccomics.com
www.marvel.com
www.barbie.com

Catalogs

Ltd. Commodities, Inc., is a catalog offering great gifts and housewares in lots of three at tremendously reduced prices. It's a wonderful source for Christmas gifts and has at least two seasonal catalogs. Their customer service number is 847-295-6058.

Oriental Trading Company, which calls itself the world's biggest toy box, is a fabulous catalog for everything you'll need for parties. They claim to have 10,000 items from goodie bags to gifts, candy, and party ware. It also has great novelty items (this is where you look for that Magic Eight Ball and lava lamps). You can call for a catalog at 1-800-228-2269 or visit their Web site at www.oriental.com

The Archie McPhee company also sells oddball toys and novelties (they're famous for their rubber chickens). You can order their catalog by calling 425-745-0711 or visit their Web site at www.mcphee.com

For craft catalogs, I would recommend doing an online search using those words. You will receive a ton of listings.

However, if you don't have Internet access, there is a catalog of catalogs called the Encyclopedia of Catalogs. They charge you for each catalog they send you (when most places will send them to you free, but you do have to know where to go for that). You can get the Encyclopedia of Catalogs by calling 561-997-1221.

Shopping

As I mentioned throughout the book, I do a tremendous amount of my party shopping at wholesale clubs. My personal preference is for Costco versus Sam's, because I find the selection there better suits my needs. Each wholesale club has its own brands.

To find a Costco nearest you, call 1-800-774-2678.

Sam's Club does not have an 800 number, but you can visit their Web site at www.wal-mart.com or call their online customer service at 1-888-SHOP-SAM.

For the BJ's closest to you, call 1-800-257-2582.

If you do not live within driving or public transportation distance of a wholesale club, you can try locating a Caldor's (1-800-Caldor-8), Kmart (www.kmart.com), Wal-Mart (www.wal-mart.com), Bradlee's (1-800-444-0171), Genovese (1-800-9-Genovese), CVS (www.cvs.com), and Osco Drug Store as well as other large retailers. They often sell items in bulk, but won't have quite the selection of a wholesale club.

In addition, you should memorize the stock at the nearest discount store. For me (as a New Yorker) these include Odd Lots and Webers. However, when I go to Maine, I always take a stroll through the local Ames, a great discount store. When I'm on the West Coast I look for a MacFrugal's or a Ross, both great discount-store chains. Some yellow pages will have listings under "discount stores."

The best dollar store in New York is Jack's 99 Cent stores. There are a number of locations in Manhattan. I know that there is a national chain of dollar stores called Dollar Bill's, and there is also a chain called Dollar Stores.

National party store chains include the Party Store (1-888-517-9369), but look up Party Stores in the business-to-business yellow pages or check the Internet for sites.

Books

The famous Pirate party for $10 is on page 103 of *The Tightwad Gazette* (New York: Villard books) by Amy Dacyczyn. It's also a great reference for all things frugal.

You might look through *The Frugal Gourmet* by Jeff Smith (New York: Avon Books) for recipe ideas (although they tend to be complicated) or browse through any of Martha Stewart's books for party ideas.

The cookbooks I use most often are: Craig Claiborne's *The New York Times Cookbook* (New York: Harper & Row), *Betty Crocker Cookbook* (New York: Golden Books), *American Cookery* by James Beard (Boston: Little, Brown), and *The Moosewood Cookbook* by Mollie Katzen (New York: 10 Speed Press). I find these have just about any basic recipe I need.

Miscellaneous

A Riese restaurant discount card, which can be used for groups or parties in certain restaurants, can be obtained by calling 1-800-399-1024. The restaurants included are T.G.I. Friday's, Charley O's, Beefsteak Charlie's, Lindy's, Martini's, Tequilaville, Sizzler, Java Shop, Houlihan's, and El Torito.

When you join this Reise Meal Ticket Reward Club, they will send you a coupon for a free meal on your birthday.

I also have a Transmedia discount card, which gives me 25 percent off at the Riese restaurants, as well as others throughout the country. It can be obtained by calling 1-800-422-1231 or by contacting Transmedia on the Internet at www.transmediacard.com There are additional discounts available at hotels and at some stores. At least twice a year they will send you a pocket-sized catalog of where the card can be used.

Index